Pop Internationalism

Pop Internationalism

Paul Krugman

The MIT Press
Cambridge, Massachusetts
London, England

Eighth printing, 1998

First MIT Press paperback edition, 1997

© 1996 Massachusetts Institute of Technology

This book was set in Palatino by Asco Trade Typesetting Ltd., Hong Kong and was printed and bound in the United States of America.

Library of Congress Cataloging-in-Publication Data

Krugman, Paul R.
 Pop internationalism / Paul Krugman.
  p.   cm.
 Includes index.
 ISBN 0-262-11210-8 (HB), 0-262-61133-3 (PB)
  1. International economic relations. 2. International trade.
I. Title.
HF1359.K784   1996
337—dc20   95-35632
                                             CIP

Contents

Introduction

I had a moment of revelation on a December's day in Little Rock, as I was listening to John Sculley.

It wasn't quite the kind of revelation that the speaker had in mind. Sculley, at the time the CEO of Apple Computer, was known for his wide-ranging speeches about the digital future; these speeches had not only given him a reputation as a technological visionary but also had made him the odds-on favorite business leader of President-elect Clinton. And so when the Administration-in-waiting held an economic summit in Little Rock, the opening remarks by MIT's Robert Solow were followed by a presentation by Sculley about the new realities of the global economy. Sculley described a world in which nations, like corporations, are engaged in fierce competition for global markets. And this vision met with obvious approval from the audience, including Bill Clinton.

But not from me. I thought I knew something about international trade, and it seemed to me that Sculley had no idea what he was talking about. (Although I didn't know it at the time, Steven Levy's book about the Macintosh computer, *Insanely Great*, suggests that many computer people felt the same about his technological visions.) The really disturbing thing, however, was that Sculley was not alone in his misunderstandings.

While some of the presentations at that conference were made by sensible, well-informed economists, a high fraction—and the ones that obviously played best both with the audience and with the new Administration—were not. That is, what was being preached in Little Rock was a kind of imitation international economics that sounded impressive and sophisticated but bore no resemblance to the real thing.

Something really strange was going on. It was as if a high-profile conference had been convened that was billed as a gathering of the world's leading experts on human psychology—and up there on the podium, giving the lead address, was John Bradshaw, telling me how to get in touch with my inner child.

But as I thought about it, I realized that the prevalence of ersatz economics in Little Rock was no accident. After all, imagine that you are an intelligent American without a background in economics who tries to keep abreast of current events—who watches the *McNeil-Lehrer Newshour*, who reads *The Atlantic* and *The New York Review of Books*—and that you have decided to bone up on international economic issues. What would you read? In chapter 5 I offer a sample reading list of seven recent books, beginning with Lester Thurow's enormously influential *Head to Head*. The books on the list share two features. They all offer a view of the world, more or less like Sculley's, of international trade as an arena of, as Thurow puts it, "win-lose" competition among nations. And they all contain little or nothing of what economists think they know about international trade. (For example, Thurow's book does not contain a single entry for "comparative advantage" in its index.)

In other words, all of the things that have been painfully learned through a couple of centuries of hard thinking about and careful study of the international economy—that tradition that reaches back to David Hume's essay, "On the balance of trade"—have been swept out of public discourse. Their place has been taken by a glib rhetoric that appeals to those who want to sound sophisticated without engaging in hard thinking; and this rhetoric has come to dominate popular discussion so completely that someone who wanted to learn about world trade without reading a textbook would probably never realize that there is anything better.

Whose fault is the replacement of serious discussion of world trade by what I have come to think of as "pop internationalism"? To some extent, of course, it is the result of basic human instincts: intellectual laziness, even among those who would be seen as wise and deep, will always be a powerful force. To some extent it also reflects the decline in the influence of economists in general: the high prestige of the profession a generation ago had much to do with the presumed effectiveness of Keynesian macroeconomic policies, and has suffered greatly as macroeconomics has dissolved into squabbling factions. And one should not ignore the role of editors, who often prefer what pop internationalists have to say to the disturbingly difficult ideas of people who know how to read national accounts or understand that the trade balance is also the difference between savings and investment. Indeed, some important editors, like James Fallows at *The Atlantic* or Robert Kuttner at *The American Prospect* are pop internationalists themselves; they deliberately use their magazines as platforms for what amounts to an anti-intellectual crusade.

But a substantial share of the blame for the rise of pop internationalism surely falls on international economists themselves, who have not tried very hard to communicate with a broader public. After all, what would you tell that intelligent American, who wants to know something about the world economy, to read? There are several pretty good textbooks out there, but they are not much fun. A few first-rate international economists, like Columbia's Jagdish Bhagwati, do write op-eds, publish articles in *The New Republic*, and appear on public TV. But the op-ed or short-article formats—let alone the three-minute TV spot—are poorly suited to presenting well-rounded ideas about the international economy, where everything affects everything else in at least two ways. And in any case, it seemed to me, after my epiphany at Little Rock, that most economists who try to write for an intellectual public presume too much; they imagine that their readers must understand, for example, that it is an accounting impossibility for Third World nations simultaneously to attract large inflows of capital and run massive trade surpluses, and thus fail to connect with an audience that is easily persuaded by authoritative-sounding men that they will do just that. (I am told on reliable hearsay that one celebrated pop internationalist remarked about his career, "Luckily, economists can't write.")

And so I came away from Little Rock with a new awareness that even the simplest, most basic truths about international trade had been driven out of public discussion. I talked about that new awareness a few weeks later, at the American Economic Association meetings; that talk appears as chapter 8. But this was the wrong audience: indeed, one journalist even mentioned the favorable reception the talk received as evidence of the stupidity and narrow-mindedness of economists. I made another attempt to express my concerns when I was asked to review Laura D'Andrea Tyson's *Who's Bashing Whom* for *The New York Review of Books*; in that review, which praised her book, I warned against the danger of confusing sophisticated revisions of international trade theory with a know-nothing rejection of any kind of systematic analysis. But the editor refused to publish the piece, telling me that "you're criticizing some very prestigious people." (The unpublished review is reproduced, unaltered, as chapter 7.)

What I eventually realized was that an effective answer to pop internationalism would require a new kind of writing. I would have to write essays for non-economists that were clear, effective, and even entertaining—otherwise, nobody would read them. The essays could not contain even a hint of technical economic jargon, because the target reader was someone who might think he knew a lot about economics but had never been exposed to the real thing. They would have to be entirely self-contained: I would have to develop their arguments from the ground up, without presuming either any prior knowledge or any appeals to the authority of my profession. And, finally, the essays would have to be *right*—no intellectual cheap shots, because after all, letting the world see what real economic analysis was like was the whole point of the exercise.

Where could I publish such essays, assuming I could write them? A good set of opportunities arose in the second half of 1993. The managing editor at *Foreign Affairs* asked me to write a piece on the then-hot debate over the North American Free Trade Agreement (reproduced as chapter 10); I countered with a proposal for a two-fer, with the NAFTA article to be followed by a piece on competitiveness. At about the same time, *Scientific American* asked me to do a piece on international trade; a little later, the *Harvard Business Review* also solicited an article. And from there, one thing led to another: it turned out that there really was an audience for serious international economics written for a broader public.

This book collects some of the articles I wrote over the two years after my revelation at Little Rock, together with a few pieces written earlier that help put those writings in context.

The first group of essays represents my assault on pop internationalism. They also represent some experimentation with styles. Chapter 1 was written to shock and provoke. It succeeded in that aim and was met with a firestorm of reaction. In particular, several leading pop internationalists responded angrily to my attack, along the way offering an almost too-good-to-be-true demonstration of the very faults—carelessness with numbers, inability to keep basic accounting straight—of which I had accused them. My response to the critics is reproduced as chapter 2. The next two essays were written in more sober styles: Robert Lawrence and I gave *Scientific American* a low-key, just-the-facts discussion of US trade, while in *Harvard Business Review* I did my best to do Economics 101 for the business reader. Finally, in chapter 5—given as a talk at the American Economic Association two years after the Little Rock summit—I tried to explain why good things have happened to bad ideas (and people).

There is, of course, a certain irony in the way that I found myself playing the role of defender of civilized economics against the intellectual barbarians. My own reputation as an economic researcher had been based largely on my role in the development of the so-called "new trade theory," which challenged some significant aspects of the theoretical paradigm that prevailed in the late 1970s. If you want a parallel to my position, it is quite a lot like that of the evolutionist Stephen Jay Gould, whose professional reputation was based on his theory of "punctuated equilibrium," the assertion that evolution proceeds in occasional spurts rather than at a constant rate. By the standards of his field, this made Gould a radical; but once he began writing for a broader public, he found that he was obliged to take on the role of defending the basic truth of evolution against the assaults of creationists.

In any case, the essays in part II represent some efforts on my part to explain how one can throw out the intellectual bathwater while saving the baby. These essays are somewhat harder going than those in part I, partly because they were written before I had realized just what getting my ideas across would require; I include them anyway, if only to show where I was coming from. Chapter 6 is a piece I wrote for *Science* at a time when I still thought that pop internationalists might be interested in serious ideas; chapter 7, my ill-fated review of Laura D'Andrea Tyson, written in the false belief that the editor of *The New York Review of Books* had some respect for my intellectual tradition; chapter 8, the talk I gave at the American Economic Association soon after the Little Rock summit.

Even as I launched my campaign against pop internationalism, there was a discernible shift in the target of that doctrine's concerns. In 1992 pop internationalists were obsessed with the perceived struggle among the great industrial powers. Over the next few years, however, debate tended instead to be focused on the effects of growth in low-wage economies. Chapter 9 is a speech I gave in Mexico City in March 1993; I like to think that it shows that I was ahead of the curve both on the politics of trade and, alas, in fearing that the euphoria, then prevalent about the prospects for the "emerging market" economies, was greatly excessive. Chapter 10 was the original *Foreign Affairs* piece, an attempt to offer a sober and realistic explanation of what NAFTA would and would not do. And chapter 11 was an attempt to widen the debate, to get people to reconsider some of their easy assumptions about Asian growth.

Finally, since the thrust of much of what I have written about international trade has been to debunk the idea that our economic fate is bound up in some kind of competitive struggle, it has also been necessary to say something about what I think really is going on. The answer, in brief, is that technological change, not global competition, is the really important story. The essays in part IV of this book represent two perspectives, once again intended to force people to think harder than they might want to.

In the end, John Sculley did me a favor. He led me to seek out and explore a new way of communicating economic ideas, to boldly go where few economists had gone before. I don't know how many people I have convinced over the last few years, but I have at least put the world on notice that pop internationalism is not all that there is. And I like to think that along the way I have provided some evidence that economists *can* write, after all.

Pop Internationalism

I A Zero-Sum World?

1

Competitiveness: A Dangerous Obsession

The Hypothesis Is Wrong

In June 1993, Jacques Delors made a special presentation to the leaders of the nations of the European Community, meeting in Copenhagen, on the growing problem of European unemployment. Economists who study the European situation were curious to see what Delors, president of the EC Commission, would say. Most of them share more or less the same diagnosis of the European problem: the taxes and regulations imposed by Europe's elaborate welfare states have made employers reluctant to create new jobs, while the relatively generous level of unemployment benefits has made workers unwilling to accept the kinds of low-wage jobs that help keep unemployment comparatively low in the United States. The monetary difficulties associated with preserving the European Monetary System in the face of the costs of German reunification have reinforced this structural problem.

It is a persuasive diagnosis, but a politically explosive one, and everyone wanted to see how Delors would handle it.

Reprinted by permission from *Foreign Affairs* (March/April 1994): 28–44. © 1994 by the Council on Foreign Relations, Inc.

Would he dare tell European leaders that their efforts to pursue economic justice have produced unemployment as an unintended by-product? Would he admit that the EMS could be sustained only at the cost of a recession and face the implications of that admission for European monetary union?

Guess what? Delors didn't confront the problems of either the welfare state or the EMS. He explained that the root cause of European unemployment was a lack of competitiveness with the United States and Japan and that the solution was a program of investment in infrastructure and high technology.

It was a disappointing evasion, but not a surprising one. After all, the rhetoric of competitiveness—the view that, in the words of President Clinton, each nation is "like a big corporation competing in the global marketplace"—has become pervasive among opinion leaders throughout the world. People who believe themselves to be sophisticated about the subject take it for granted that the economic problem facing any modern nation is essentially one of competing on world markets— that the United States and Japan are competitors in the same sense that Coca-Cola competes with Pepsi—and are unaware that anyone might seriously question that proposition. Every few months a new best-seller warns the American public of the dire consequences of losing the "race" for the 21st century.[1] A whole industry of councils on competitiveness, "geo-economists" and managed trade theorists has sprung up in Washington. Many of these people, having diagnosed America's economic problems in much the same terms as Delors did Europe's, are now in the highest reaches of the Clinton administration formulating economic and trade policy for the United States. So Delors was using a language that was not only convenient but comfortable for him and a wide audience on both sides of the Atlantic.

Unfortunately, his diagnosis was deeply misleading as a guide to what ails Europe, and similar diagnoses in the United

States are equally misleading. The idea that a country's economic fortunes are largely determined by its success on world markets is a hypothesis, not a necessary truth; and as a practical, empirical matter, that hypothesis is flatly wrong. That is, it is simply not the case that the world's leading nations are to any important degree in economic competition with each other, or that any of their major economic problems can be attributed to failures to compete on world markets. The growing obsession in most advanced nations with international competitiveness should be seen, not as a well-founded concern, but as a view held in the face of overwhelming contrary evidence. And yet it is clearly a view that people very much want to hold—a desire to believe that is reflected in a remarkable tendency of those who preach the doctrine of competitiveness to support their case with careless, flawed arithmetic.

This article makes three points. First, it argues that concerns about competitiveness are, as an empirical matter, almost completely unfounded. Second, it tries to explain why defining the economic problem as one of international competition is nonetheless so attractive to so many people. Finally, it argues that the obsession with competitiveness is not only wrong but dangerous, skewing domestic policies and threatening the international economic system. This last issue is, of course, the most consequential from the standpoint of public policy. Thinking in terms of competitiveness leads, directly and indirectly, to bad economic policies on a wide range of issues, domestic and foreign, whether it be in health care or trade.

Mindless Competition

Most people who use the term "competitiveness" do so without a second thought. It seems obvious to them that the analogy between a country and a corporation is reasonable and that to ask whether the United States is competitive in the world market is no different in principle from asking whether General Motors is competitive in the North American minivan market.

In fact, however, trying to define the competitiveness of a nation is much more problematic than defining that of a corporation. The bottom line for a corporation is literally its bottom line: if a corporation cannot afford to pay its workers, suppliers, and bondholders, it will go out of business. So when we say that a corporation is uncompetitive, we mean that its market position is unsustainable—that unless it improves its performance, it will cease to exist. Countries, on the other hand, do not go out of business. They may be happy or unhappy with their economic performance, but they have no well-defined bottom line. As a result, the concept of national competitiveness is elusive.

One might suppose, naively, that the bottom line of a national economy is simply its trade balance, that competitiveness can be measured by the ability of a country to sell more abroad than it buys. But in both theory and practice a trade surplus may be a sign of national weakness, a deficit a sign of strength. For example, Mexico was forced to run huge trade surpluses in the 1980s in order to pay the interest on its foreign debt since international investors refused to lend it any more money; it began to run large trade deficits after 1990 as foreign investors recovered confidence and began to pour in new funds. Would anyone want to describe Mexico as a highly competitive nation during the debt crisis era or describe what has happened since 1990 as a loss in competitiveness?

Most writers who worry about the issue at all have therefore tried to define competitiveness as the combination of favorable trade performance and something else. In particular, the most popular definition of competitiveness nowadays runs along the lines of the one given in Council of Economic Advisors Chairman Laura D'Andrea Tyson's *Who's Bashing Whom?*: competitiveness is "our ability to produce goods and services that meet the test of international competition while our citizens enjoy a standard of living that is both rising and sustainable." This sounds reasonable. If you think about it, however, and test your thoughts against the facts, you will find out that there is much less to this definition than meets the eye.

Consider, for a moment, what the definition would mean for an economy that conducted very little international trade, like the United States in the 1950s. For such an economy, the ability to balance its trade is mostly a matter of getting the exchange rate right. But because trade is such a small factor in the economy, the level of the exchange rate is a minor influence on the standard of living. So in an economy with very little international trade, the growth in living standards—and thus "competitiveness" according to Tyson's definition—would be determined almost entirely by domestic factors, primarily the rate of productivity growth. That's domestic productivity growth, period—not productivity growth relative to other countries. In other words, for an economy with very little international trade, "competitiveness" would turn out to be a funny way of saying "productivity" and would have nothing to do with international competition.

But surely this changes when trade becomes more important, as indeed it has for all major economies? It certainly could change. Suppose that a country finds that although its productivity is steadily rising, it can succeed in exporting only if it repeatedly devalues its currency, selling its exports ever more cheaply on world markets. Then its standard of living, which depends on its purchasing power over imports as well as domestically produced goods, might actually decline. In the jargon of economists, domestic growth might be outweighed by deteriorating terms of trade.[2] So "competitiveness" could turn out really to be about international competition after all.

There is no reason, however, to leave this as a pure speculation; it can easily be checked against the data. Have deteriorating terms of trade in fact been a major drag on the U.S.
standard of living? Or has the rate of growth of U.S. real
income continued essentially to equal the rate of domestic productivity growth, even though trade is a larger share of income
than it used to be?

To answer this question, one need only look at the national
income accounts data the Commerce Department publishes
regularly in the *Survey of Current Business*. The standard measure of economic growth in the United States is, of course, real
GNP—a measure that divides the value of goods and services
produced in the United States by appropriate price indexes to
come up with an estimate of real national output. The Commerce Department also, however, publishes something called
"command GNP." This is similar to real GNP except that it
divides U.S. exports not by the export price index, but by
the price index for U.S. imports. That is, exports are valued
by what Americans can buy with the money exports bring.
Command GNP therefore measures the volume of goods and
services the U.S. economy can "command"—the nation's purchasing power—rather than the volume it produces.[3] And as
we have just seen, "competitiveness" means something different
from "productivity" if and only if purchasing power grows
significantly more slowly than output.

Well, here are the numbers. Over the period 1959–73, a
period of vigorous growth in U.S. living standards and few
concerns about international competition, real GNP per worker-
hour grew 1.85 percent annually, while command GNP per
hour grew a bit faster, 1.87 percent. From 1973 to 1990, a
period of stagnating living standards, command GNP growth
per hour slowed to 0.65 percent. Almost all (91 percent)
of that slowdown, however, was explained by a decline in

domestic productivity growth: real GNP per hour grew only 0.73 percent.

Similar calculations for the European Community and Japan yield similar results. In each case, the growth rate of living standards essentially equals the growth rate of domestic productivity—not productivity relative to competitors, but simply domestic productivity. Even though world trade is larger than ever before, national living standards are overwhelmingly determined by domestic factors rather than by some competition for world markets.

How can this be in our interdependent world? Part of the answer is that the world is not as interdependent as you might think: countries are nothing at all like corporations. Even today, U.S. exports are only 10 percent of the value-added in the economy (which is equal to GNP). That is, the United States is still almost 90 percent an economy that produces goods and services for its own use. By contrast, even the largest corporation sells hardly any of its output to its own workers; the "exports" of General Motors—its sales to people who do not work there—are virtually all of its sales, which are more than 2.5 times the corporation's value-added.

Moreover, countries do not compete with each other the way corporations do. Coke and Pepsi are almost purely rivals: only a negligible fraction of Coca-Cola's sales go to Pepsi workers, only a negligible fraction of the goods Coca-Cola workers buy are Pepsi products. So if Pepsi is successful, it tends to be at Coke's expense. But the major industrial countries, while they sell products that compete with each other, are also each other's main export markets and each other's main suppliers of useful imports. If the European economy does well, it need not be at U.S. expense; indeed, if anything a successful European economy is likely to help the U.S. economy by providing it with larger markets and selling it goods of superior quality at lower prices.

International trade, then, is not a zero-sum game. When productivity rises in Japan, the main result is a rise in Japanese real wages; American or European wages are in principle at least as likely to rise as to fall, and in practice seem to be virtually unaffected.

It would be possible to belabor the point, but the moral is clear: while competitive problems could arise in principle, as a practical, empirical matter the major nations of the world are not to any significant degree in economic competition with each other. Of course, there is always a rivalry for status and power—countries that grow faster will see their political rank rise. So it is always interesting to *compare* countries. But asserting that Japanese growth diminishes U.S. status is very different from saying that it reduces the U.S. standard of living—and it is the latter that the rhetoric of competitiveness asserts.

One can, of course, take the position that words mean what we want them to mean, that all are free, if they wish, to use the term "competitiveness" as a poetic way of saying productivity, without actually implying that international competition has anything to do with it. But few writers on competitiveness would accept this view. They believe that the facts tell a very different story, that we live, as Lester Thurow put it in his best-selling book, *Head to Head*, in a world of "win-lose" competition between the leading economies. How is this belief possible?

Careless Arithmetic

One of the remarkable, startling features of the vast literature on competitiveness is the repeated tendency of highly intelligent authors to engage in what may perhaps most tactfully be described as "careless arithmetic." Assertions are made that sound like quantifiable pronouncements about measurable magnitudes, but the writers do not actually present any data on these magnitudes and thus fail to notice that the actual numbers contradict their assertions. Or data are presented that are supposed to support an assertion, but the writer fails to notice that his own numbers imply that what he is saying cannot be true. Over and over again one finds books and articles on competitiveness that seem to the unwary reader to be full of convincing evidence but that strike anyone familiar with the data as strangely, almost eerily inept in their handling of the numbers. Some examples can best illustrate this point. Here are three cases of careless arithmetic, each of some interest in its own right.

Trade Deficits and the Loss of Good Jobs. In a recent article published in Japan, Lester Thurow explained to his audience the importance of reducing the Japanese trade surplus with the United States. U.S. real wages, he pointed out, had fallen six percent during the Reagan and Bush years, and the reason was that trade deficits in manufactured goods had forced workers out of high-paying manufacturing jobs into much lower-paying service jobs.

This is not an original view; it is very widely held. But Thurow was more concrete than most people, giving actual numbers for the job and wage loss. A million manufacturing jobs have been lost because of the deficit, he asserted, and manufacturing jobs pay 30 percent more than service jobs.

Both numbers are dubious. The million-job number is too high, and the 30 percent wage differential between manufacturing and services is primarily due to a difference in the length of the workweek, not a difference in the hourly wage rate. But let's grant Thurow his numbers. Do they tell the story he suggests?

The key point is that total U.S. employment is well over 100 million workers. Suppose that a million workers were forced from manufacturing into services and as a result lost the 30 percent manufacturing wage premium. Since these workers are less than 1 percent of the U.S. labor force, this would reduce the average U.S. wage rate by less than 1/100 of 30 percent— that is, by less than 0.3 percent.

This is too small to explain the 6 percent real wage decline *by a factor of 20*. Or to look at it another way, the annual wage loss from deficit-induced deindustrialization, which Thurow clearly implies is at the heart of U.S. economic difficulties, is on the basis of his own numbers roughly equal to what the U.S. spends on health care every week.

Something puzzling is going on here. How could someone as intelligent as Thurow, in writing an article that purports to offer hard quantitative evidence of the importance of international competition to the U.S. economy, fail to realize that the evidence he offers clearly shows that the channel of harm that he identifies was *not* the culprit?

High Value-added Sectors. Ira Magaziner and Robert Reich, both now influential figures in the Clinton Administration, first reached a broad audience with their 1982 book, *Minding America's Business*. The book advocated a U.S. industrial policy, and in the introduction the authors offered a seemingly concrete quantitative basis for such a policy: "Our standard of living can only rise if (i) capital and labor increasingly flow to industries with high value-added per worker and (ii) we maintain a position in those industries that is superior to that of our competitors."

Economists were skeptical of this idea on principle. If targeting the right industries was simply a matter of moving into sectors with high value-added, why weren't private markets already doing the job?[4] But one might dismiss this as simply the usual boundless faith of economists in the market; didn't Magaziner and Reich back their case with a great deal of real-world evidence?

Well, *Minding America's Business* contains a lot of facts. One thing it never does, however, is actually justify the criteria set out in the introduction. The choice of industries to cover clearly implied a belief among the authors that high value-added is more or less synonymous with high technology, but nowhere in the book do any numbers compare actual value-added per worker in different industries.

Such numbers are not hard to find. Indeed, every public library in America has a copy of the *Statistical Abstract of the United States*, which each year contains a table presenting value-added and employment by industry in U.S. manufacturing. All one needs to do, then, is spend a few minutes in the library with a calculator to come up with a table that ranks U.S. industries by value-added per worker.

The table on this page shows selected entries from pages 740–744 of the 1991 *Statistical Abstract*. It turns out that the U.S. industries with really high value-added per worker are in sectors with very high ratios of capital to labor, like cigarettes and petroleum refining. (This was predictable: because capital-intensive industries must earn a normal return on large investments, they must charge prices that are a larger markup over

Table 1.1
Value added per worker, 1988 (in thousands of dollars)

Cigarettes	488
Petroleum refining	283
Autos	99
Steel	97
Aircraft	68
Electronics	64
All manufacturing	66

labor costs than labor-intensive industries, which means that they have high value-added per worker). Among large industries, value-added per worker tends to be high in traditional heavy manufacturing sectors like steel and autos. High-technology sectors like aerospace and electronics turn out to be only roughly average.

This result does not surprise conventional economists. High value-added per worker occurs in sectors that are highly capital-intensive, that is, sectors in which an additional dollar of capital buys little extra value-added. In other words, there is no free lunch.

But let's leave on one side what the table says about the way the economy works, and simply note the strangeness of the lapse by Magaziner and Reich. Surely they were not calling for an industrial policy that would funnel capital and labor into the steel and auto industries in preference to high-tech. How, then, could they write a whole book dedicated to the proposition that we should target high value-added industries without ever checking to see which industries they meant?

Labor Costs. In his own presentation at the Copenhagen summit, British Prime Minister John Major showed a chart indicating that European unit labor costs have risen more rapidly than those in the United States and Japan. Thus he argued that European workers have been pricing themselves out of world markets.

But a few weeks later Sam Brittan of the *Financial Times* pointed out a strange thing about Major's calculations: the labor costs were not adjusted for exchange rates. In international competition, of course, what matters for a U.S. firm are the costs of its overseas rivals measured in dollars, not marks or yen. So international comparisons of labor costs, like the tables the Bank of England routinely publishes, always convert them into a common currency. The numbers presented by

Major, however, did not make this standard adjustment. And it was a good thing for his presentation that they didn't. As Brittan pointed out, European labor costs have not risen in relative terms when the exchange rate adjustment is made.

If anything, this lapse is even odder than those of Thurow or Magaziner and Reich. How could John Major, with the sophisticated statistical resources of the U.K. Treasury behind him, present an analysis that failed to make the most standard of adjustments?

These examples of strangely careless arithmetic, chosen from among dozens of similar cases, by people who surely had both the cleverness and the resources to get it right, cry out for an explanation. The best working hypothesis is that in each case the author or speaker wanted to believe in the competitive hypothesis so much that he felt no urge to question it; if data were used at all, it was only to lend credibility to a predetermined belief, not to test it. But why are people apparently so anxious to define economic problems as issues of international competition?

The Thrill of Competition

The competitive metaphor—the image of countries competing with each other in world markets in the same way that corporations do—derives much of its attractiveness from its seeming comprehensibility. Tell a group of businessmen that a country is like a corporation writ large, and you give them the comfort of feeling that they already understand the basics. Try to tell them about economic concepts like comparative advantage, and you are asking them to learn something new. It should not be surprising if many prefer a doctrine that offers the gain of apparent sophistication without the pain of hard thinking. The rhetoric of competitiveness has become so wide-spread, however, for three deeper reasons.

First, competitive images are exciting, and thrills sell tickets. The subtitle of Lester Thurow's huge best-seller, *Head to Head*, is "The Coming Economic Battle among Japan, Europe, and America"; the jacket proclaims that "the decisive war of the century has begun... and America may already have decided to lose." Suppose that the subtitle had described the real situation: "The coming struggle in which each big economy will succeed or fail based on its own efforts, pretty much independently of how well the others do." Would Thurow have sold a tenth as many books?

Second, the idea that U.S. economic difficulties hinge crucially on our failures in international competition somewhat paradoxically makes those difficulties seem easier to solve. The productivity of the average American worker is determined by a complex array of factors, most of them unreachable by any likely government policy. So if you accept the reality that our "competitive" problem is really a domestic productivity problem pure and simple, you are unlikely to be optimistic about any dramatic turnaround. But if you can convince yourself that the problem is really one of failures in international competition—that imports are pushing workers out of high-wage jobs, or subsidized foreign competition is driving the United States out of the high value-added sectors—then the answers to economic malaise may seem to you to involve simple things like subsidizing high technology and being tough on Japan.

Finally, many of the world's leaders have found the competitive metaphor extremely useful as a political device. The rhetoric of competitiveness turns out to provide a good way either to justify hard choices or to avoid them. The example of Delors in Copenhagen shows the usefulness of competitive metaphors as an evasion. Delors had to say something at the EC summit; yet to say anything that addressed the real roots of European unemployment would have involved huge political risks. By turning the discussion to essentially irrelevant but plausible-sounding questions of competitiveness, he bought himself some time to come up with a better answer (which to some extent he provided in December's white paper on the European economy—a paper that still, however, retained "competitiveness" in its title).

By contrast, the well-received presentation of Bill Clinton's initial economic program in February 1993 showed the usefulness of competitive rhetoric as a motivation for tough policies. Clinton proposed a set of painful spending cuts and tax increases to reduce the Federal deficit. Why? The real reasons for cutting the deficit are disappointingly undramatic: the deficit siphons off funds that might otherwise have been productively invested, and thereby exerts a steady if small drag on U.S. economic growth. But Clinton was able instead to offer a stirring patriotic appeal, calling on the nation to act now in order to make the economy competitive in the global market—with the implication that dire economic consequences would follow if the United States does not.

Many people who know that "competitiveness" is a largely meaningless concept have been willing to indulge competitive rhetoric precisely because they believe they can harness it in the service of good policies. An overblown fear of the Soviet Union was used in the 1950s to justify the building of the interstate highway system and the expansion of math and science education. Cannot the unjustified fears about foreign competition similarly be turned to good, used to justify serious efforts to reduce the budget deficit, rebuild infrastructure, and so on?

A few years ago this was a reasonable hope. At this point, however, the obsession with competitiveness has reached the point where it has already begun dangerously to distort economic policies.

The Dangers of Obsession

Thinking and speaking in terms of competitiveness poses three real dangers. First, it could result in the wasteful spending of government money supposedly to enhance U.S. competitiveness. Second, it could lead to protectionism and trade wars. Finally, and most important, it could result in bad public policy on a spectrum of important issues.

During the 1950s, fear of the Soviet Union induced the U.S. government to spend money on useful things like highways and science education. It also, however, led to considerable spending on more doubtful items like bomb shelters. The most obvious if least worrisome danger of the growing obsession with competitiveness is that it might lead to a similar misallocation of resources. To take an example, recent guidelines for government research funding have stressed the importance of supporting research that can improve U.S. international competitiveness. This exerts at least some bias toward inventions that can help manufacturing firms, which generally compete on international markets, rather than service producers, which generally do not. Yet most of our employment and value-added is now in services, and lagging productivity in services rather than manufactures has been the single most important factor in the stagnation of U.S. living standards.

A much more serious risk is that the obsession with competitiveness will lead to trade conflict, perhaps even to a world trade war. Most of those who have preached the doctrine of competitiveness have not been old-fashioned protectionists. They want their countries to win the global trade game, not drop out. But what if, despite its best efforts, a country does not seem to be winning, or lacks confidence that it can? Then the competitive diagnosis inevitably suggests that to close the borders is better than to risk having foreigners take away high-wage jobs and high-value sectors. At the very least, the focus on the supposedly competitive nature of international economic relations greases the rails for those who want confrontational if not frankly protectionist policies.

We can already see this process at work, in both the United States and Europe. In the United States, it was remarkable how quickly the sophisticated interventionist arguments advanced by Laura Tyson in her published work gave way to the simple-minded claim by U.S. Trade Representative Mickey Kantor that Japan's bilateral trade surplus was costing the United States millions of jobs. And the trade rhetoric of President Clinton, who stresses the supposed creation of high-wage jobs rather than the gains from specialization, left his administration in a weak position when it tried to argue with the claims of NAFTA foes that competition from cheap Mexican labor will destroy the U.S. manufacturing base.

Perhaps the most serious risk from the obsession with competitiveness, however, is its subtle indirect effect on the quality of economic discussion and policymaking. If top government officials are strongly committed to a particular economic doctrine, their commitment inevitably sets the tone for policymaking on all issues, even those which may seem to have nothing to do with that doctrine. And if an economic doctrine is flatly, completely and demonstrably wrong, the insistence that discussion adhere to that doctrine inevitably blurs the focus and diminishes the quality of policy discussion across a broad range of issues, including some that are very far from trade policy per se.

Consider, for example, the issue of health care reform, undoubtedly the most important economic initiative of the Clinton administration, almost surely an order of magnitude more important to U.S. living standards than anything that might be done about trade policy (unless the United States provokes a full-blown trade war). Since health care is an issue with few direct international linkages, one might have expected it to be largely insulated from any distortions of policy resulting from misguided concerns about competitiveness.

But the administration placed the development of the health care plan in the hands of Ira Magaziner, the same Magaziner who so conspicuously failed to do his homework in arguing for government promotion of high value-added industries. Magaziner's prior writings and consulting on economic policy focused almost entirely on the issue of international competition, his views on which may be summarized by the title of his 1990 book, *The Silent War*. His appointment reflected many factors, of course, not least his long personal friendship with the first couple. Still, it was not irrelevant that in an administration committed to the ideology of competitiveness Magaziner, who has consistently recommended that national industrial policies be based on the corporate strategy concepts he learned during his years at the Boston Consulting Group, was regarded as an economic policy expert.

We might also note the unusual process by which the health care reform was developed. In spite of the huge size of the task force, recognized experts in the health care field were almost completely absent, notably though not exclusively economists specializing in health care, including economists with impeccable liberal credentials like Henry Aaron of the Brookings Institution. Again, this may have reflected a number of factors, but it is probably not irrelevant that anyone who, like Magaziner, is strongly committed to the ideology of competitiveness is bound to have found professional economists notably unsympathetic in the past—and to be unwilling to deal with them on any other issue.

To make a harsh but not entirely unjustified analogy, a government wedded to the ideology of competitiveness is as unlikely to make good economic policy as a government committed to creationism is to make good science policy, even in areas that have no direct relationship to the theory of evolution.

Advisers with No Clothes

If the obsession with competitiveness is as misguided and damaging as this article claims, why aren't more voices saying so? The answer is, a mixture of hope and fear.

On the side of hope, many sensible people have imagined that they can appropriate the rhetoric of competitiveness on behalf of desirable economic policies. Suppose that you believe that the United States needs to raise its savings rate and improve its educational system in order to raise its productivity. Even if you know that the benefits of higher productivity have nothing to do with international competition, why not describe this as a policy to enhance competitiveness if you think that it can widen your audience? It's tempting to pander to popular prejudices on behalf of a good cause, and I have myself succumbed to that temptation.

As for fear, it takes either a very courageous or very reckless economist to say publicly that a doctrine that many, perhaps most, of the world's opinion leaders have embraced is flatly wrong. The insult is all the greater when many of those men and women think that by using the rhetoric of competitiveness they are demonstrating their sophistication about economics. This article may influence people, but it will not make many friends.

Unfortunately, those economists who have hoped to appropriate the rhetoric of competitiveness for good economic policies have instead had their own credibility appropriated on behalf of bad ideas. And somebody has to point out when the emperor's intellectual wardrobe isn't all he thinks it is.

So let's start telling the truth: competitiveness is a meaningless word when applied to national economies. And the obsession with competitiveness is both wrong and dangerous.

Notes

1. See, for just a few examples, Laura D'Andrea Tyson, *Who's Bashing Whom: Trade Conflict in High-Technology Industries*, Washington: Institute for International Economics, 1992; Lester C. Thurow, *Head to Head: The Coming Economic Battle among Japan, Europe, and America*, New York: Morrow, 1992; Ira C. Magaziner and Robert B. Reich, *Minding America's Business: The Decline and Rise of the American Economy*, New York: Vintage Books, 1983; Ira C. Magaziner and Mark Patinkin, *The Silent War: Inside the Global Business Battles Shaping America's Future*, New York: Vintage Books, 1990; Edward N. Luttwak, *The Endangered American Dream: How to Stop the United States from Becoming a Third World Country and How to Win the Geo-economic Struggle for Industrial Supremacy*, New York: Simon and Schuster, 1993; Kevin P. Phillips, *Staying on Top: The Business Case for a National Industrial Strategy*, New York: Random House, 1984; Clyde V. Prestowitz, Jr., *Trading Places: How We Allowed Japan to Take the Lead*, New York: Basic Books, 1988; William S. Dietrich, *In the Shadow of the Rising Sun: The Political Roots of American Economic Decline*, University Park: Pennsylvania State University Press, 1991; Jeffrey E. Garten, *A Cold Peace: America, Japan, Germany, and the Struggle for Supremacy*, New York: Times Books, 1992; and Wayne Sandholtz et al., *The Highest Stakes: The Economic Foundations of the Next Security System*, Berkeley Roundtable on the International Economy (BRIE), Oxford University Press, 1992.

2. An example may be helpful here. Suppose that a country spends 20 percent of its income on imports, and that the price of its imports are set not in domestic but in foreign currency. Then if the country is forced to devalue its currency—reduce its value in foreign currency—by 10 percent, this will raise the price of 20 percent of the country's spending basket by 10 percent, thus raising the overall price index by 2 percent. Even if domestic *output* has not changed, the country's real *income* will therefore have fallen by 2 percent. If the

country must repeatedly devalue in the face of competitive pressure, growth in real income will persistently lag behind growth in real output.

It's important to notice, however, that the size of this lag depends not only on the amount of devaluation but on the share of imports in spending. A 10 percent devaluation of the dollar against the yen does not reduce U.S. real income by 10 percent—in fact, it reduces U.S. real income by only about 0.2 percent because only about 2 percent of U.S. income is spent on goods produced in Japan.

3. In the example in the previous footnote, the devaluation would have no effect on real GNP, but command GNP would have fallen by two percent. The finding that in practice command GNP has grown almost as fast as real GNP therefore amounts to saying that events like the hypothetical case in footnote two are unimportant in practice.

4. "Value-added" has a precise, standard meaning in national income accounting: the value added of a firm is the dollar value of its sales, minus the dollar value of the inputs it purchases from other firms, and as such it is easily measured. Some people who use the term, however, may be unaware of this definition and simply use "high value-added" as a synonym for "desirable."

My article in the March/April issue of *Foreign Affairs* has obviously upset many people. Some of my critics claim that I misrepresented their position, that despite their insistent use of the word "competitiveness" they have never believed that the major industrial nations are engaged in a competitive economic struggle. Others claim that I have gotten the economics wrong: that countries *are* engaged in a competitive struggle. Indeed, some of them make both claims in the same response.

Moving Target

Lester C. Thurow vigorously denies ever asserting that international competition is a central issue for the U.S. economy. In particular, he cites page counts from his 1985 book, *The Zero-Sum Solution*, to demonstrate that domestic factors are his principal concern. But Thurow's most recent book is *Head to Head*, which follows its provocative title with the subtitle, *The Coming Battle Among Japan, Europe and America*. The book jacket asserts that the "decisive war of the century has begun." The

Reprinted by permission from *Foreign Affairs* (July/August 1994): 198–203. © 1994 by the Council on Foreign Relations, Inc.

text asserts over and over that the major economic powers are now engaged in "win-lose" competition for world markets, a competition that has taken the place of the military competition between East and West. Thurow now says that international strategic competition is no more than seven percent of the problem; did the typical reader of *Head to Head* get this message?

Similarly, Stephen S. Cohen denies that he, or indeed anyone else with whom I should "deign to take difference," has ever said the things I claim competitiveness advocates believe. But in 1987 Cohen, together with John Zysman, published *Manufacturing Matters*, a book that seemed to say two (untrue) things: the long-term downward trend in the share of manufacturing in U.S. employment is largely due to foreign competition, and this declining share is a major economic problem.

After their initial denial, both Cohen and Thurow proceed to argue that international competition is of crucial importance after all. In this they are joined by Clyde V. Prestowitz, Jr., who at least makes no bones about believing that trade and trade policy are the central issue for the U.S. economy. Does Cohen believe that Prestowitz—or James Fallows, who expressed similar views in his new book, *Looking at the Sun*—is one of those people with whom I should not deign to argue?

Sloppy Math: Part II

Of all the elements in my article, the section on careless arithmetic—the strange pattern of errors in reporting or using data in articles and books on competitiveness—has enraged the most people. Both Thurow and Prestowitz have taken care to fill their responses with a blizzard of numbers and calculations. However, some of the numbers are puzzling.

For example, Thurow says that imports are 14 percent of U.S. GNP, while exports are only 10 percent, and that reducing imports to equal exports would add $250 billion to the sales of U.S. manufacturers. But according to *Economic Indicators*, the monthly statistical publication of the Joint Economic Committee, U.S. imports in 1993 were only 11.4 percent of GDP, while exports were 10.4 percent. Even the current account deficit, a broader measure that includes some additional debit items, was only $109 billion. If the United States were to cut imports by $250 billion, far from merely balancing its trade as Thurow asserts, the United States would run a current account *surplus* of $140 billion—that is, more than the 2 percent maximum of GDP U.S. negotiators have demanded Japan set as a target!

Or consider Prestowitz, who derides my claim that high-technology industries, commonly described as "high value" sectors, actually have much lower value added per worker than traditional "high volume," heavy industrial sectors. I have aggregated too much by looking at broad sectors like electronics, he says; I should look at the highest-tech lines of business, like semiconductors, where value added per worker is $234,000. Prestowitz should report the results of his research to the Department of Commerce, whose staff has obviously incorrectly calculated (in the *Annual Survey of Manufactures*) that in 1989 value added per worker in Standard Industrial Classification 3674 (semiconductors and related devices) was $96,487—closer to the $76,709 per worker in SIC 2096 (potato chips and related snacks) than to the $187,569 in SIC 3711 (motor vehicles and car bodies).[1]

Everyone makes mistakes, although it is surprising when men who are supposed to be experts on international competition do not have even a rough idea of the size of the U.S. trade deficit or know how to look up a standard industrial statistic.

The interesting point, however, is that the mistakes made by Thurow, Prestowitz and other competitiveness advocates are not random errors; they are always biased in the same direction. That is, the advocates always err in a direction that makes international competition seem more important than it really is.

Beyond these petty, if revealing, errors of fact are a series of conceptual misunderstandings. For example, Prestowitz argues that productivity in sectors that compete on world markets is much more important than productivity in non-traded service sectors because the former determine wage rates throughout the economy. For example, because U.S. manufacturing workers are much more productive than their Third World counterparts, U.S. barbers, who do not have a comparable productivity advantage, also get high wages. But Prestowitz fails to notice that the converse is also true: service productivity affects the real wages of manufacturing workers. Because the high relative productivity of U.S. manufacturing is not matched in the haircut sector, haircuts by those well-paid barbers are much more expensive than haircuts in the Third World; as a result real wages of U.S. manufacturing workers (that is, wages in terms of what they can buy, including haircuts) are not as high as they would be if U.S. barbers were more productive. With careful thought, one realizes that real wages depend on the overall productivity of the economy, with no special presumption that productivity in manufacturing—or in internationally traded sectors in general—deserves any more attention or active promotion than productivity elsewhere.

Cohen makes essentially the same mistake when he complains that I underestimated the effects of competitive pressure because I focused only on import and export prices and did not consider the further impacts of that pressure on profits and wages. He somehow fails to realize that a change in wages or profits that is not reflected in import or export prices cannot change overall U.S. real income—it can only redistribute profits to one group within the United States at the expense of another. That is why the effect of international price competition on U.S. real income can be measured by the change in the ratio of export to import prices—full stop. And the effects of changes in this ratio on the U.S. economy have, as I showed in my article, been small.

Or consider Thurow's analysis of the benefits that would accrue to the United States if it could roll back imports (leaving aside the inaccuracy of his numbers). He asserts that the United States could create five million new jobs in import-competing sectors, and he assumes that all five million jobs represent a net addition to employment. But this assumption is unrealistic. As this reply was being written, the Federal Reserve was raising interest rates in an effort to rein in a recovery that it feared would proceed too far, that is, lead to excessive employment, producing a renewed surge in inflation. Some people think that the Fed is tightening too soon, but the essential point is that the growth of employment is not determined by the ability of the United States to sell goods on world markets or to compete with imports, but by the Fed's judgement of what will not set off inflation. So suppose that the United States were to impose import quotas, adding millions of jobs in import-competing sectors. The Fed would respond by raising interest rates to prevent an overheated economy, and most if not all of the job gains would be matched by job losses elsewhere.

Things Add Up

In each of these cases, my critics seem to have forgotten the most basic principle of economics: things add up. Higher employment in import-competing industries must come either through a reduction in unemployment, in which case one must ask whether the implied unemployment rate (about three percent in Thurow's example) is feasible, or at the expense of jobs elsewhere in the economy, in which case no overall job gain takes place. If higher manufacturing wages lead to a higher wage rate for barbers without higher tonsorial productivity, the gain must come at someone else's expense. Since it is hard to see how foreigners pay for more expensive American haircuts, that wage gain can only redistribute the benefits of manufacturing productivity from one set of American workers to another, not increase the total gains. In their haste to assign great importance to international competition, my critics, like the inventors of perpetual motion machines, have failed to realize that there are conservation principles that any story about the economy must honor.

But perhaps Cohen, Thurow and Prestowitz stumble on economic basics because they are so eager to get to their main point, which is that advanced economic theory, and in particular the theory of strategic trade policy, supports their obsession with competitiveness.

Prestowitz's central assertion is that the theory of strategic trade policy, which he for some reason thinks I invented in a paper about aircraft competition (the actual inventors were James Brander and Barbara Spencer, who never mentioned aircraft), justifies aggressively interventionist trade policies. He further asserts that economists in general, and I in particular, have run away from that implication for ideological reasons.

Well, that's not quite the real story. It is true that in the early 1980s professional economists became aware that one of the implications of new theories of international trade was a possible role for strategic policies to promote exports in certain industries. Confronted with a new idea that was exciting, potentially important but untested, these economists began a sustained process of research, probing the weak points, confronting the new idea with the data. After all, lots of things could be true in principle. For example in certain theoretical situations a tax cut could definitely stimulate the economy so much that government revenues would actually rise, and it would be very nice if that were the actual situation; but unfortunately it isn't. Similarly, it is definitely possible to imagine a situation in which, because of all of the market imperfections Thurow dwells on, a clever strategic trade policy would sharply raise U.S. real income. And it would be very nice if the United States could devise such a policy. But is that possibility really there? To answer that question requires looking hard at the facts.

And so over the course of the last ten years a massive international research program has explored the prospects for strategic trade policy.[2] Two broad conclusions emerge. First, to identify which industries should receive strategic promotion or the appropriate form and level of promotion is very difficult. Second, the payoffs of even a successful strategic trade policy are likely to be very modest—certainly far less even than Thurow's "seven percent solution," which is closer to the entire share of international trade in the U.S. economy.

Research results are always open to challenge, especially in an inexact field like economics. If Prestowitz wants to point out specific failings in the dozens of painstaking empirical studies of strategic trade that have been carried out over the past decade, by all means let him do so. His remarks about the subject, however, strongly suggest that while he is happy to mention strategic trade theory in support of his policy writing, Prestowitz has not read any of the economic literature.

I do, however, agree with Prestowitz on one point. More people should read the works of Friedrich List. If they do, they may wonder why this turgid, confused writer—whose theory led him to predict that Holland and Denmark would be condemned to permanent economic backwardness unless they sought political union with Germany—has suddenly become a favorite of Fallows, Prestowitz and others. The new cult of List bears an uncanny resemblance to the right-wing supply-siders' canonization of the classical French economist Jean-Baptiste Say, who claimed that the economy as a whole could never suffer from the falls in aggregate demand that produce recessions.[3] The motive of the supply-siders was, of course, to cover simplistic ideas with a veneer of faux scholarship.

In contrast to Prestowitz and Thurow, who offer coherent if flawed reasons to worry about international competition, Cohen offers a more difficult target. Basically, he asks us to accept "competitiveness" as a kind of ineffable essence that cannot be either defined or measured. Data that seem to suggest the importance of this essence are cited as "indicators," whatever that means, while those that do not are dismissed as unreliable. Both in his article and other writings he has persistently used a rhetoric that seems to portray international trade as a game with winners and losers, but when challenged on any particular point he denies having said it. I guess I don't understand how a concept so elusive can be a useful guide to policy.

My original article in *Foreign Affairs* argued that a doctrine that views world trade as a competitive struggle has become widely accepted, that this view is wrong but that there is nonetheless an intense desire to believe in that doctrine. The article enraged many, especially when it asserted that the desire to believe in competitive struggle repeatedly leads highly intelligent authors into surprising lapses in their handling of concepts and data. I could not, however, have asked for a better demonstration of my point than the responses published in this issue.

Notes

1. I don't know why Thurow thinks the U.S. trade deficit is four times as big as it actually is. I have, however, tracked down Prestowitz's number. It is not value added per employee; it is shipments (which are always larger than value added) divided by the number of production workers (who are only a fraction of total employment, especially in high-technology industries).

2. The original paper on strategic trade policy was James Brander and Barbara Spencer, "Export Subsidies and International Market Share Rivalry," *Journal of International Economics*, February 1985, pp. 83–100. See also Paul Krugman, ed., *Strategic Trade Policy and the New International Economics*, Cambridge: MIT Press, 1986; Robert Feenstra, ed., *Empirical Methods for International Trade*, Chicago: University of Chicago Press, 1988; Robert Baldwin, ed., *Trade Policy Issues and Empirical Analysis*, Chicago: University of Chicago Press, 1988; and Paul Krugman and Alasdair Smith, eds., *Empirical Studies of Strategic Trade Policy*, Chicago: University of Chicago Press, 1994.

3. Fallows officially evaluated List to guru status in his article "How the World Works," *The Atlantic Monthly*, December 1993, pp. 60–87. Readers may wish to compare the elevation of Say by Jude Wanniski in his influential supply-side tract, *The Way the World Works*, New York: Basic Books, 1978.

3   Trade, Jobs, and Wages

The real wage of the average American worker more than doubled between the end of World War II and 1973. Since then, however, those wages have risen only 6 percent. Furthermore, only highly educated workers have seen their compensation rise; the real earnings of blue-collar workers have fallen in most years since 1973.

Why have wages stagnated? A consensus among business and political leaders attributes the problem in large part to the failure of the U.S. to compete effectively in an increasingly integrated world economy. This conventional wisdom holds that foreign competition has eroded the U.S. manufacturing base, washing out the high-paying jobs that a strong manufacturing sector provides. More broadly, the argument goes, the nation's real income has lagged as a result of the inability of many U.S. firms to sell in world markets. And because imports increasingly come from Third World countries with their huge reserves of unskilled labor, the heaviest burden of this foreign competition has ostensibly fallen on less educated American workers.

Reprinted by permission from *Scientific American* (April 1994): 22–27. © 1994 by Scientific American, Inc. All rights reserved.

Many people find such a story extremely persuasive. It links America's undeniable economic difficulties to the obvious fact of global competition. In effect, the U.S. is (in the words of President Bill Clinton) "like a big corporation in the world economy"—and, like many big corporations, it has stumbled in the face of new competitive challenges.

Persuasive though it may be, however, that story is untrue. A growing body of evidence contradicts the popular view that international competition is central to U.S. economic problems. In fact, international factors have played a surprisingly small role in the country's economic difficulties. The manufacturing sector has become a smaller part of the economy, but international trade is not the main cause of that shrinkage. The growth of real income has slowed almost entirely for domestic reasons. And—contrary to what even most economists have believed—recent analyses indicate that growing international trade does not bear significant responsibility even for the declining real wages of less educated U.S. workers.

The fraction of U.S. workers employed in manufacturing has been declining steadily since 1950. So has the share of U.S. output accounted for by value added in manufacturing. (Measurements of "value added" deduct from total sales the cost of raw materials and other inputs that a company buys from other firms.) In 1950 value added in the manufacturing sector accounted for 29.6 percent of gross domestic product (GDP) and 34.2 percent of employment; in 1970 the shares were 25.0 and 27.3 percent, respectively; by 1990 manufacturing had fallen to 18.4 percent of GDP and 17.4 percent of employment.

Before 1970 those who worried about this trend generally blamed it on automation—that is, on rapid growth of productivity in manufacturing. Since then, it has become more common to blame deindustrialization on rising imports; indeed, from 1970 to 1990, imports rose from 11.4 to 38.2 percent of the manufacturing contribution to GDP.

Yet the fact that imports grew while industry shrank does not in itself demonstrate that international competition was responsible. During the same 20 years, manufacturing exports also rose dramatically, from 12.6 to 31.0 percent of value added. Many manufacturing firms may have laid off workers in the face of competition from abroad, but others have added workers to produce for expanding export markets.

To assess the overall impact of growing international trade on the size of the manufacturing sector, we need to estimate the net effect of this simultaneous growth of exports and imports. A dollar of exports adds a dollar to the sales of domestic manufacturers; a dollar of imports, to a first approximation, displaces a dollar of domestic sales. The net impact of trade on domestic manufacturing sales can therefore be measured simply by the manufacturing trade balance—the difference between the total amount of manufactured goods that the U.S. exports and the amount that it imports. (In practice, a dollar of imports may displace slightly less than a dollar of domestic sales because the extra spending may come at the expense of services or other nonmanufacturing sales. The trade balance sets an upper bound on the net effect of trade on manufacturing.)

Undoubtedly, the emergence of persistent trade deficits in manufactured goods has contributed to the declining share of manufacturing in the U.S. economy. The question is how large that contribution has been. In 1970 manufactured exports exceeded imports by 0.2 percent of GDP. Since then, there have been persistent deficits, reaching a maximum of 3.1 percent of GDP in 1986. By 1990, however, the manufacturing deficit had fallen again, to only 1.3 percent of GDP. The decline in the

U.S. manufacturing trade position over those two decades was only 1.5 percent of GDP, less than a quarter of the 6.6 percentage point decline in the share of manufacturing in GDP.

Moreover, the raw value of the trade deficit overstates its actual effect on the manufacturing sector. Trade figures measure sales, but the contribution of manufacturing to GDP is defined by value added in the sector—that is, by sales minus purchases from other sectors. When imports displace a dollar of domestic manufacturing sales, a substantial fraction of that dollar would have been spent on inputs from the service sector, which are not part of manufacturing's contribution to GDP.

To estimate the true impact of the trade balance on manufacturing, one must correct for this "leakage" to the service sector. Our analysis of data from the U.S. Department of Commerce puts the figure at 40 percent. In other words, each dollar of trade deficit reduces the manufacturing sector's contribution to GDP by only 60 cents. This adjustment strengthens our conclusion: if trade in manufactured goods had been balanced from 1970 to 1990, the downward trend in the size of the manufacturing sector would not have been as steep as it actually was, but most of the deindustrialization would still have taken place. Between 1970 and 1990 manufacturing declined from 25.0 to 18.4 percent of GDP; with balanced trade, the decline would have been from 24.9 to 19.2, about 86 percent as large.

International trade explains only a small part of the decline in the relative importance of manufacturing to the economy. Why, then, has the share of manufacturing declined? The immediate reason is that the composition of domestic spending has shifted away from manufactured goods. In 1970 U.S. residents spent 46 percent of their outlays on goods (manufactured, grown or mined) and 54 percent on services and construction. By 1991 the shares were 40.7 and 59.3 percent,

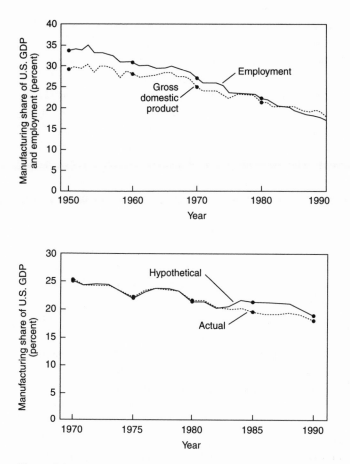

Figure 3.1
Manufacturing share of gross domestic product has declined during the post-war era. The sector's share of domestic employment has decreased even more rapidly (above). Even if the U.S. were not importing more manufactured goods than it exports, however, correcting for trade balance shows that most of the decline would still have taken place (below).

respectively, as people began buying comparatively more health care, travel, entertainment, legal services, fast food and so on. It is hardly surprising, given this shift, that manufacturing has become a less important part of the economy.

In particular, U.S. residents are spending a smaller fraction of their incomes on goods than they did 20 years ago for a simple reason: goods have become relatively cheaper. Between 1970 and 1990 the price of goods relative to services fell 22.9 percent. The physical ratio of goods to services purchased remained almost constant during that period. Goods have become cheaper primarily because productivity in manufacturing has grown much faster than in services. This growth has been passed on in lower consumer prices.

Ironically, the conventional wisdom here has things almost exactly backward. Policymakers often ascribe the declining share of industrial employment to a lack of manufacturing competitiveness brought on by inadequate productivity growth. In fact, the shrinkage is largely the result of high productivity growth, at least as compared with the service sector. The concern, widely voiced during the 1950s and 1960s, that industrial workers would lose their jobs because of automation is closer to the truth than the current preoccupation with a presumed loss of manufacturing jobs because of foreign competition.

Because competition from abroad has played a minor role in the contraction of U.S. manufacturing, loss of jobs in this sector because of foreign competition can bear only a tiny fraction of the blame for the stagnating earnings of U.S. workers. Our data illuminate just how small that fraction is. In 1990, for example, the trade deficit in manufacturing was $73 billion. This deficit reduced manufacturing value added by approximately $42 billion (the other $31 billion represents leakage— goods and services that manufacturers would have purchased from other sectors). Given an average of about $60,000 value added per manufacturing employee, this figure corresponded to approximately 700,000 jobs that would have been held by U.S. workers. In that year, the average manufacturing worker earned about $5,000 more than the average nonmanufacturing worker. Assuming that any loss of manufacturing jobs was made up by a gain of nonmanufacturing jobs—an assumption borne out by the absence of any long-term upward trend in the U.S. unemployment rate—the loss of "good jobs" in manufacturing as a result of international competition corresponded to a loss of $3.5 billion in wages. U.S. national income in 1990 was $5.5 trillion; consequently, the wage loss from deindustrialization in the face of foreign competition was less than 0.07 percent of national income.

Many observers have expressed concern not just about wages lost because of a shrinking manufacturing sector but also about a broader erosion of U.S. real income caused by inability to compete effectively in world markets. But they often fail to make the distinction between the adverse consequences of having slow productivity growth—which would be bad even for an economy that did not have any international trade—and additional adverse effects that might result from productivity growth that lags behind that of other countries.

To see why that distinction is important, consider a world in which productivity (output per worker-hour) increases by the same amount in every nation around the world—say, 3 percent a year. Under these conditions, all other things remaining equal, workers' real earnings in all countries would tend to rise by 3 percent annually as well. Similarly, if productivity grew at 1 percent a year, so would earnings. (The relation between productivity growth and earnings growth holds regardless of the absolute level of productivity in each nation; only the rate of increase is significant.)

Concerns about international competitiveness, as opposed to low productivity growth, correspond to a situation in which productivity growth in the U.S. falls to 1 percent annually while elsewhere it continues to grow at 3 percent. If real earnings in the U.S. then grow at 1 percent a year, the U.S. does not have anything we could reasonably call a competitive problem, even though it would lag other nations. The rate of earnings growth is exactly the same as it would be if other countries were doing as badly as we are.

The fact that other countries are doing better may hurt U.S. pride, but it does not by itself affect domestic standards. It makes sense to talk of a competitive problem only to the extent that earnings growth falls by more than the decline in productivity growth.

Foreign competition can reduce domestic income by a well-understood mechanism called the terms of trade effect. In export markets, foreign competition can force a decline in the prices of U.S. products relative to those of other nations. That decline typically occurs through a devaluation of the dollar, thereby boosting the price of imports. The net result is a reduction in real earnings because the U.S. must sell its goods more cheaply and pay more for what it buys.

During the past 20 years, the U.S. has indeed experienced a deterioration in its terms of trade. The ratio of U.S. export prices to import prices fell more than 20 percent between 1970 and 1990; in other words, the U.S. had to export 20 percent more to pay for a given quantity of imports in 1990 than it did in 1970. Because the U.S. imported goods whose value was 11.3 percent of its GDP in 1990, these worsened terms of trade reduced national income by about 2 percent.

Real earnings grew by about 6 percent during the 1970s and 1980s. Our calculation suggests that avoiding the decline in the terms of trade would have increased that growth to only about 8 percent. Although the effect of foreign competition is measurable, it can by no means account for the stagnation of U.S. earnings.

A more direct way of calculating the impact of the terms of trade on real income is to use a measure known as command GNP (gross national product). Real GNP, the conventional standard of economic performance, measures what the output of the economy would be if all prices remained constant. Command GNP is a similar measure in which the value of exports is deflated by the import price index. It measures the quantity of goods and services that the U.S. economy can afford to buy in the world market, as opposed to the volume of goods and services it produces. If the prices of imports rise faster than export prices (as will happen, for example, if the dollar falls precipitously), growth in command GNP will fall behind that of real GNP.

Between 1959 and 1973, when U.S. wages were rising steadily, command GNP per worker-hour did grow slightly faster than real GNP per hour—1.87 percent per year versus 1.85. Between 1973 and 1990, as real wages stagnated, command GNP grew more slowly than output, 0.65 percent versus 0.73. Both these differences, however, are small. The great bulk of the slowdown in command GNP was caused by the slower growth of real GNP per worker—by the purely domestic impact of the decline in productivity growth.

If foreign competition is neither the main villain in the decline of manufacturing nor the root cause of stagnating wages, has it not at least worsened the lot of unskilled labor? Economists have generally been quite sympathetic to the argument that increased integration of global markets has pushed down the real wages of less educated U.S. workers.

Their opinion stems from a familiar concept in the theory of international trade: factor price equalization. When a rich country, where skilled labor is abundant (and where the premium

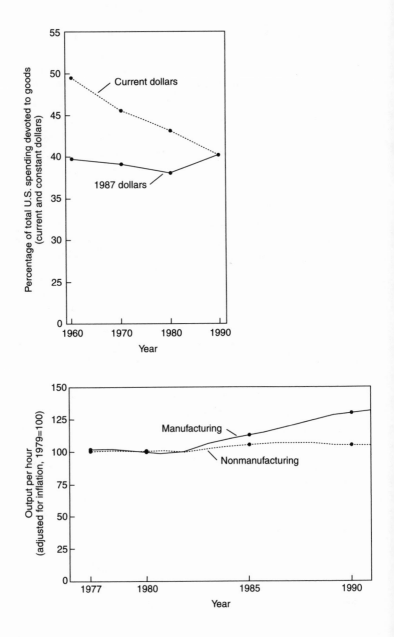

for skill is therefore small), trades with a poor country, where skilled workers are scarce and unskilled workers abundant, the wage rates tend to converge. The pay of skilled workers rises in the rich country and falls in the poor one; that of unskilled workers falls in the rich country and rises in the poor nation.

Given the rapid growth of exports from nations such as China and Indonesia, it seems reasonable to suppose that factor price equalization has been a major reason for the growing gap in earnings between skilled and unskilled workers in the U.S. Surprisingly, however, this does not seem to be the case. We have found that increased wage inequality, like the decline of manufacturing and the slowdown in real income growth, is overwhelmingly the consequence of domestic causes.

That conclusion is based on an examination of the evidence in terms of the underlying logic of factor price equalization, first explained in a classic 1941 paper by Wolfgang F. Stolper and Paul A. Samuelson. The principle of comparative advantage suggests that a rich country trading with a poor one will export skill-intensive goods (because it has a comparative abundance of skilled workers) and import labor-intensive products. As a result of this trade, production in the rich country will shift toward skill-intensive sectors and away from labor-intensive ones. That shift, however, raises the demand for skilled workers and reduces that for unskilled workers. If wages are free to rise and fall with changes in the demand for different kinds of labor (as they do for the most part in the U.S.), the real wages of skilled workers will rise, and those of unskilled workers will decline. In a poor country, the opposite will occur.

◀ **Figure 3.2**
Share of U.S. domestic spending going to manufactured goods has declined substantially since 1960, although the volume of goods purchased has not (above). Instead goods have simply become cheaper relative to services. Productivity growth in the manufacturing sector has far outpaced such growth in service industries, especially during the past 10 years (below).

All other things being equal, the rising wage differential will lead firms in the rich country to cut back on the proportion of skilled workers that they employ and to increase that of unskilled ones. That decision, in turn, mitigates the increased demand for skilled workers. When the dust settles, the wage differential has risen just enough to offset the effects of the change in the industry mix on overall demand for labor. Total employment of both types of labor remains unchanged.

According to Stolper and Samuelson's analysis, a rising relative wage for skilled workers leads all industries to employ a lower ratio of skilled to unskilled workers. Indeed, this reduction is the only way the economy can shift production toward skill-intensive sectors while keeping the overall mix of workers constant.

This analysis carries two clear empirical implications. First, if growing international trade is the main force driving increased wage inequality, the ratio of skilled to unskilled employment should decline in most U.S. industries. Second, employment should increase more rapidly in skill-intensive industries than in those that employ more unskilled labour.

Recent U.S. economic history confounds these predictions. Between 1979 and 1989 the real compensation of white-collar workers rose, whereas that of blue-collar workers fell. Nevertheless, nearly all industries employed an increasing proportion of white-collar workers. Moreover, skill-intensive industries showed at best a slight tendency to grow faster than those in which blue-collar employment was high. (Although economists use many different methods to estimate the average skill level in a given industrial sector, the percentage of blue-collar workers is highly correlated with other measures and easy to estimate.)

Thus, the evidence suggests that factor price equalization was not the driving force behind the growing wage gap. The rise in demand for skilled workers was overwhelmingly caused by changes in demand *within* each industrial sector, not by a shift of the U.S.'s industrial mix in response to trade. No one can say with certainty what has reduced the relative demand for less skilled workers throughout the economy. Technological change, especially the increased use of computers, is a likely candidate; in any case, globalization cannot have played the dominant role.

It may seem difficult to reconcile the evidence that international competition bears little responsibility for falling wages among unskilled workers with the dramatic rise in manufactured exports from Third World countries. In truth, however, there is little need to do so. Although the surging exports of some developing countries have attracted a great deal of attention, the U.S. continues to buy the bulk of its imports from other advanced countries, whose workers have similar skills and wages. In 1990 the average wages of manufacturing workers among U.S. trading partners (weighted by total bilateral trade) were 88 percent of the U.S. level. Imports (other than oil) from low-wage countries—those where workers earn less than half the U.S. level—were a mere 2.8 percent of GDP.

Finally, increasing low-wage competition from trade with developing nations has been offset by the rise in wages and skill levels among traditional U.S. trading partners. Indeed, imports from low-wage countries were almost as large in 1960 as in 1990—2.2 percent of GDP—because three decades ago Japan and most of Europe fell into that category. In 1960 imports from Japan exerted competitive pressure on labor-intensive industries such as textiles. Today Japan is a high-wage country, and the burden of its competition falls mostly on skill-intensive sectors such as the semiconductor industry.

We have examined the case for the havoc supposedly wrought by foreign competition and found it wanting. Imports are not responsible for the stagnation of U.S. incomes since 1973, nor for deindustrialization, nor for the plight of low-wage workers. That does not mean, however, we believe all is well.

Some of those who have raised the alarm about U.S. competitiveness seem to believe only two positions are possible: either the U.S. has a competitive problem, or else the nation's economy is performing acceptably. We agree that the U.S. economy is doing badly, but we find that international competition explains very little of that poor performance.

The sources of U.S. difficulties are overwhelmingly domestic, and the nation's plight would be much the same even if world markets had not become more integrated. The share of manufacturing in GDP is declining because people are buying relatively fewer goods; manufacturing employment is falling because companies are replacing workers with machines and making more efficient use of those they retain. Wages have stagnated because the rate of productivity growth in the economy as a whole has slowed, and less skilled workers in particular are suffering because a high-technology economy has less and less demand for their services. Our trade with the rest of the world plays at best a small role in each case.

The data underlying our conclusions are neither subtle nor difficult to interpret. The evidence that international trade has had little net impact on the size of the manufacturing sector, in particular, is blatant. The prevalence of contrary views among opinion leaders who believe themselves well informed says something disturbing about the quality of economic discussion in this country.

It is important to get these things right. Improving American economic performance is an arduous task. It will be an impossible one if we start from the misconceived notion that our problem is essentially one of international competitiveness.

4   Does Third World Growth Hurt First World Prosperity?

Only a short while ago, our most influential business writers were warning that the biggest threat to U.S. prosperity was competition from other developed countries. One need only look at the subtitle of Lester Thurow's 1992 best-seller, *Head to Head: The Coming Economic Battle Among Japan, Europe, and America*. But in the last year or so, our supposed economic adversaries have begun to appear a lot less invincible: both the Japanese and the German economies are stuck in intractable recessions, their exports hammered by overvalued currencies and their vaunted labor-market institutions fraying under the impact of economic adversity. In comparison, the U.S. economy, while hardly a picture of glowing prosperity, looks healthy.

But even as many economic writers and corporate executives lose interest in the much-hyped U.S.–Japanese battle, they see a new battle on the horizon—between the advanced economies and the emerging economies of the Third World. There is a striking contrast between the disappointing performance of the advanced nations over the past 20 years and the successes of an increasing number of developing countries.

Reprinted by permission from *Harvard Business Review* (July/August 1994): 113–121.

Rapid economic growth, which first began in a few small Asian nations in the 1960s, has now spread across a wide arc of East Asia—not only to relatively well-off Southeast Asian nations like Malaysia and Thailand but also to two poor countries with huge populations: Indonesia and China. There are signs of similarly rapid growth in Chile and perhaps in northern Mexico; centers of rapid development, like the Bangalore software complex, are appearing even in India.

One might have expected everyone to welcome this change in the global landscape, to see the rapid improvement in the living standards of hundreds of millions of people, many of whom had previously been desperately poor, as progress—and as an unprecedented business opportunity. Rather than taking satisfaction in global economic development, however, more and more influential people in the West are regarding economic growth in the Third World as a threat.

These new fears are exemplified in a letter circulated early this year by Klaus Schwab, president of the World Economic Forum, which hosts the famous Davos conferences. Schwab asked a large number of people to provide input for a document he had been asked to prepare for UN secretary general Boutros Boutros-Ghali, entitled "Redefining the Basic Assumptions of Mankind." To indicate what he had in mind, Schwab offered a sample redefinition. Traditionally, he wrote, the world was divided into rich countries with high productivity and high wages and poor countries with low productivity and low wages. But now, he noted, some countries combine high productivity with low wages. The growing presence of those countries in world markets is leading, Schwab argued, to a "massive redeployment of productive assets," which is making it impossible for advanced nations to maintain their standards of living. In other words, competition from the emerging economies of the Third World has become a threat, perhaps *the* threat, to the economies of the First World.

Schwab's views are not unique. No less imposing a figure than Jacques Delors, president of the European Commission, seems to share them. The European Commission's eagerly awaited white paper on European economic difficulties, "Growth, Competitiveness, and Employment," released in December 1993, lists four reasons for the long upward trend in European unemployment rates. According to the report, the most important factor is the rise of nations that are "competing with us—even in our own markets—at cost levels that we simply cannot match": Eurospeak for low-wage competition from the Third World.

Such views are less widespread in the United States. In spite of the Clinton administration's tendency to define economic problems in competitive terms, it has saved its fire for advanced nations like Japan; the 1994 *Economic Report of the President* argues that imports from the Third World have not been a major pressure on the U.S. labor market, at least not so far. Still, such economic writers as *Business Week's* Robert Kuttner and think tanks like the Economic Policy Institute maintain a steady drumbeat of warnings about the threat that low-wage imports pose to U.S. living standards. The magazine *CEO/International Strategies*, in its December 1993/January 1994 issue, which was devoted to the theme "Redefining the Global Economy," published not one but three pieces on the threat of low-wage competition from developing countries. Some informal polling of noneconomists I know suggests that a majority of them, including many who consider themselves well informed about economic affairs, consider it an established fact that competition from the Third World is a major source of current U.S. economic problems.

The truth, however, is that fears about the economic impact of Third World competition are almost entirely unjustified. Economic growth in low-wage nations is in principle as likely to raise as to lower per capita income in high-wage countries;

the actual effects have been negligible. In theory, there are some reasons for concern about the possible impact of Third World competition on the *distribution* (as opposed to the *level*) of income in the West, but there are few signs that such concern is justified in practice, at least so far.

How can so many sophisticated people be so wrong? (And how can I be so sure that they are wrong?) To make sense of the alleged threat from the Third World, it is necessary to begin with a brief discussion of the world economy.

Thinking about the World Economy

The idea that Third World competition threatens living standards in advanced countries seems straightforward. Suppose that somebody has learned to do something that used to be my exclusive specialty. Maybe he or she isn't quite as good at it as I am but is willing to work for a fraction of my wage. Isn't it obvious that I am either going to have to accept a lower standard of living or be out of a job? That, in essence, is the view of those who fear that Western wage rates must fall as the Third World develops.

But this story is completely misleading. When world productivity rises (as it does when Third World countries converge on First World productivity), *average* world living standards must rise: after all, the extra output must go somewhere. This by itself creates a presumption that higher Third World productivity will be reflected in higher Third World wages, not lower First World incomes. Another way to look at it is to notice that in a national economy, producers and consumers are the same people; foreign competitors who cut prices may lower the wage I receive, but they also raise the purchasing power of whatever I earn. There is no reason to expect the adverse effect to predominate.

The world economy is a system—a complex web of feed-back relationships—not a simple chain of one-way effects. In this global economic system, wages, prices, trade, and invest-ment flows are outcomes, not givens. Intuitively plausible scenarios based on day-to-day business experience can be deeply misleading about what happens to this system when underlying parameters change, whether the parameters are government policies like tariffs and taxes or more mysterious factors like the productivity of Chinese labor.

As anyone knows who has studied a complex system, be it global weather, Los Angeles traffic patterns, or the flow of materials through a manufacturing process, it is necessary to build a model to understand how the system works. The usual procedure is to start with a very simplified model and then make it increasingly realistic; in the process, one comes to a more sophisticated understanding of the actual system.

In this article, I will follow that procedure to think about the impact of emerging economies on wages and jobs in the ad-vanced world. I will start with an oversimplified and unrealistic picture of the world economy and then gradually add realistic complications. At each stage, I will also bring in some data. By the end, I hope to have made clear that the seemingly sophisticated view that the Third World is causing First World problems is questionable on conceptual grounds and wholly implausible in terms of the data.

Model 1: A One-Good, One-Input World

Imagine a world without the complexities of the global econ-omy. In this world, one all-purpose good is produced—let's call it chips—using one input, labor. All countries produce chips, but labor is more productive in some countries than in others. In imagining such a world, we ignore two crucial facts about the actual global economy: it produces hundreds of thousands of distinct goods and services, and it does so using many inputs, including physical capital and the "human capital" that results from education.

What would determine wages and standards of living in such a simplified world? In the absence of capital or differentiation between skilled and unskilled labor, workers would receive what they produce. That is, the annual real wage in terms of chips in each country would equal the number of chips each worker produced in a year—his or her productivity. And since chips are the only good consumed as well as the only good produced, the consumer price index would contain nothing but chips. Each country's real wage rate in terms of its CPI would also equal the productivity of labor in each country.

What about relative wages? The possibility of arbitrage, of shipping goods to wherever they command the highest price, would keep chip prices the same in all countries. Thus the wage rate of workers who produce 10,000 chips annually would be ten times that of workers who produce 1,000, even if those workers are in different countries. The ratio of any two nations' wage rates, then, would equal the ratio of their workers' productivity.

What would happen if countries that previously had low productivity and thus low wages were to experience a large increase in their productivity? These emerging economies would see their wage rates in terms of chips rise—end of story. There would be no impact, positive or negative, on real wage rates in other, initially higher-wage countries. In each country, the real wage rate equals domestic productivity in terms of chips; that remains true, regardless of what happens elsewhere.

What's wrong with this model? It's ridiculously oversimplified, but in what ways might the simplification mislead us? One immediate problem with the model is that it leaves no room for international trade: if everyone is producing chips, there is no reason to import or export them. (This issue does not seem to bother such competitiveness theorists as Lester Thurow. The central proposition of Thurow's *Head to Head* is that because the advanced nations produce the same things, the benign niche competition of the past has given way to win-lose head-to-head competition. But if the advanced nations are producing the same things, why do they sell so much to one another?)

While the fact that countries do trade with one another means that our simplified model cannot be literally true, this model does raise the question of how extensive the trade actually is between advanced nations and the Third World. It turns out to be surprisingly small despite the emphasis on Third World trade in such documents as the Delors white paper. In 1990, advanced industrial nations spent only 1.2% of their combined GDPs on imports of manufactured goods from newly industrializing economies. A model in which advanced countries have no reason to trade with low-wage countries is obviously not completely accurate, but it is more than 98% right all the same.

Another problem with the model is that without capital, there can be no international investment. We'll come back to that point when we put capital into the model. It's worth noting, however, that in the U.S. economy, more than 70% of national income accrues to labor and less than 30% to capital; this proportion has been very stable for the past two decades. Labor is clearly not the only input in the production of goods, but the assertion that the average real wage rate moves almost one for one with output per worker, that what is good for the United States is good for U.S. workers and vice versa, seems approximately correct.

One last assertion that may bother some readers is that wages automatically rise with productivity. Is this realistic?

Yes. Economic history offers no example of a country that experienced long-term productivity growth without a roughly equal rise in real wages. In the 1950s, when European productivity was typically less than half of U.S. productivity, so were European wages; today average compensation measured in dollars is about the same. As Japan climbed the productivity ladder over the past 30 years, its wages also rose, from 10% to 110% of the U.S. level. South Korea's wages have also risen dramatically over time. Indeed, many Korean economists worry that wages may have risen too much. Korean labor now seems too expensive to compete in low-technology goods with newcomers like China and Indonesia and too expensive to compensate for low productivity and product quality in such industries as autos.

The idea that somehow the old rules no longer apply, that new entrants on the world economic stage will always pay low wages even as their productivity rises to advanced-country levels, has no basis in actual experience. (Some economic writers try to refute this proposition by pointing to particular industries in which relative wages don't match relative productivity. For example, shirtmakers in Bangladesh, who are almost half as productive as shirtmakers in the United States, receive far less than half the U.S. wage rate. But as we'll see when we turn to a multigood model, that is exactly what standard economic theory predicts.)

Our one-good, one-input model may seem silly, but it forces us to notice two crucial points. First, an increase in Third World labor productivity means an increase in world output, and an increase in world output must show up as an increase in *somebody's* income. And it does: it shows up in higher wages for Third World workers. Second, whatever we may eventually conclude about the impact of higher Third World productivity on First World economies, it won't necessarily be adverse. The simplest model suggests that there is no impact at all.

Model 2: Many Goods, One Input

In the real world, of course, countries specialize in the production of a limited range of goods; international trade is both the cause and the result of that specialization. In particular, the trade in manufactured goods between the First and Third worlds is largely an exchange of sophisticated high-technology products like aircraft and microprocessors for labor-intensive goods like clothing. In a world in which countries produce different goods, productivity gains in one part of the world may either help or hurt the rest of the world.

This is by no means a new subject. Between the end of World War II and the Korean War, many nations experienced a series of balance-of-payments difficulties, which led to the perception of a global "dollar shortage." At the time, many Europeans believed that their real problem was the overwhelming competitiveness of the highly productive U.S. economy. But was the U.S. economy really damaging the rest of the world? More generally, does productivity growth in one country raise or lower real incomes in other countries? An extensive body of theoretical and empirical work concluded that the impact of productivity growth abroad on domestic welfare can be either positive or negative, depending on the *bias* of that productivity growth—that is, depending on the sectors in which such growth occurs.[1]

Sir W. Arthur Lewis, who won the 1979 Nobel Prize in economics for his work on economic development, has offered a clever illustration of how the effect of productivity growth in developing countries on the real wages in advanced nations can work either way. In Lewis's model, the world is divided into two regions; call them North and South. This global economy produces not one but three types of goods: high-tech, medium-tech, and low-tech. As in our first model, however, labor is still the only input into production. Northern labor is more productive than Southern labor in all three types of goods, but that productivity advantage is huge in high-tech, moderate in medium-tech, and small in low-tech.

What will be the pattern of wages and production in such a world? A likely outcome is that high-tech goods will be produced only in the North, low-tech goods only in the South, and both regions will produce at least some medium-tech goods. (If world demand for high-tech products is very high, the North may produce only those goods; if demand for low-tech products is high, the South may also specialize. But there will be a wide range of cases in which both regions produce medium-tech goods.)

Competition will ensure that the ratio of the wage rate in the North to that in the South will equal the ratio of Northern to Southern productivity in the sector in which workers in the two regions face each other head-to-head: medium-tech. In this case, Northern workers will not be competitive in low-tech goods in spite of their higher productivity because their wage rates are too high. Conversely, low Southern wage rates are not enough to compensate for low productivity in high-tech.

A numerical example may be helpful here. Suppose that Northern labor is ten times as productive as Southern labor in high-tech, five times as productive in medium-tech, but only twice as productive in low-tech. If both countries produce medium-tech goods, the Northern wage must be five times higher than the Southern. Given this wage ratio, labor costs in the South for low-tech goods will be only two-fifths of labor costs in the North for this sector, even though Northern labor is more productive. In high-tech goods, by contrast, labor costs will be twice as high in the South.

Notice that in this example, Southern low-tech workers receive only one-fifth the Northern wage, even though they are half as productive as Northern workers in the same industry.

Many people, including those who call themselves experts on international trade, believe that kind of gap shows that conventional economic models don't apply. In fact, it's exactly what conventional analysis predicts: if low-wage countries didn't have lower unit labor costs than high-wage countries in their export industries, they couldn't export.

Now suppose that there is an increase in Southern productivity. What effect will it have? It depends on which sector experiences the productivity gain. If the productivity increase occurs in low-tech output, a sector that does not compete with Northern labor, there is no reason to expect the ratio of Northern to Southern wages to change. Southern labor will produce low-tech goods more cheaply, and the fall in the price of those goods will raise real wages in the North. But if Southern productivity rises in the competitive medium-tech sector, relative Southern wages will rise. Since productivity has not risen in low-tech production, low-tech prices will rise and *reduce* real wages in the North.

What happens if Southern productivity rises at equal rates in low- and medium-tech? The relative wage rate will rise but will be offset by the productivity increase. The prices of low-tech goods in terms of Northern labor will not change, and thus the real wages of Northern workers will not change either. In other words, an across-the-board productivity increase in the South in this multigood model has the same effect on Northern living standards as productivity growth had in the one-good model: none at all.

It seems, then, that the effect of Third World growth on the First World, which was negligible in our simplest model, becomes unpredictable once we make the model more realistic. There are, however, two points worth noting.

First, the way in which growth in the Third World can hurt the First World is very different from the way it is described in the Schwab letter or the Delors White Paper. Third World growth does not hurt the First World because wages in the Third World stay low but because they rise and therefore push up the prices of exports to advanced countries. That is, the United States may be threatened when South Korea gets better at producing automobiles, not because the United States loses the automobile market, but because higher South Korean wages mean that U.S. consumers pay more for the pajamas and toys that they were already buying from South Korea.

Second, this potential adverse effect should show up in a readily measured economic statistic: the *terms of trade*, or the ratio of export to import prices. For example, if U.S. companies are forced to sell goods more cheaply on world markets because of foreign competition or are forced to pay more for imports because of competition for raw materials or a devalued dollar, real income in the United States will fall. Because exports and imports are about 10% of GNP, each 10% decline in the U.S. terms of trade reduces U.S. real income by about 1%. The potential damage to advanced economies from Third World growth rests on the possibility of a decline in advanced-country terms of trade. But that hasn't happened. Between 1982 and 1992, the terms of trade of the developed market economies actually improved by 12%, largely as a result of falling real oil prices.

In sum, a multigood model offers more possibilities than the simple one-good model with which we began, but it leads to the same conclusion: productivity growth in the Third World leads to higher wages in the Third World, end of story.

Model 3: Capital and International Investment

Let's move a step closer to reality and add another input to our model. What changes if we now imagine a world in which production requires both capital and labor? From a global point of view, there is one big difference between labor and capital: the degree of international mobility. Although large-scale international migration was a major force in the world economy before 1920, since then all advanced countries have erected high legal barriers to economically motivated immigration. There is a limited flow of very highly skilled people from South to North—the notorious "brain drain"—and a somewhat larger flow of illegal migration. But most labor does not move internationally.

In contrast, international investment is a highly visible and growing influence on the world economy. During the late 1970s, many banks in advanced countries lent large sums of money to Third World countries. This flow dried up in the 1980s, the decade of the debt crisis, but considerable capital flows resumed with the emerging-markets boom that began after 1990.

Many of the fears about Third World growth seem to focus on capital flows rather than trade. Schwab's fear that there will be a "massive redeployment of productive assets" presumably refers to investment in the Third World. The famous estimate by the Economic Policy Institute that NAFTA would cost 500,000 U.S. jobs was based on a completely hypothetical scenario about diversion of U.S. investment. Even Labor Secretary Robert Reich, at the March 1994 job summit in Detroit, attributed the employment problems of Western economies to the mobility of capital. In effect, he seemed to be asserting that First World capital now creates only Third World jobs. Are those fears justified?

The short answer is yes in principle but no in practice. As a matter of standard textbook theory, international flows of capital from North to South could lower Northern wages. The actual flows that have taken place since 1990, however, are far

too small to have the devastating impacts that many people
envision.

To understand how international investment flows could
pose problems for advanced-country labor, we must first realize that the productivity of labor depends in part on how much
capital it has to work with. As an empirical matter, the share
of labor in domestic output is very stable. But if labor has less
capital at its disposal, productivity and thus real wage rates will
fall.

Suppose, then, that Third World nations become more attractive than First World nations for First World investors. This
might be because a change in political conditions makes such
investments seem safer or because technology transfer raises
the potential productivity of Third World workers (once they
are equipped with adequate capital). Does this hurt First World
workers? Of course. Capital exported to the Third World is
capital not invested at home, so such North-South investment
means that Northern productivity and wages will fall. Northern investors presumably earn a higher return on these investments than they could have earned at home, but that may offer
little comfort to workers.

Before we jump to the conclusion that the development
of the Third World has come at First World expense, however,
we must ask not merely whether economic damage arises in
principle but how large it is in practice.

How much capital has been exported from advanced countries to developing countries? During the 1980s, there was
essentially no net North-South investment—indeed, interest
payments and debt repayments were consistently larger than
the new investment. All the action, then, has taken place since
1990. In 1993, the peak year of emerging-markets investment
so far, capital flows from all advanced nations to all newly
industrializing countries totaled about $100 billion.

That may sound very high, but compared with the First World economy, it isn't. Last year, the combined GNPs of North America, Western Europe, and Japan totaled more than $18 trillion. Their combined investment was more than $3.5 trillion; their combined capital stocks were about $60 trillion. The record capital flows of 1993 diverted only about 3% of First World investment away from domestic use and reduced the growth in the capital stock by less than 0.2%. The entire emerging-market investment boom since 1990 has reduced the advanced world's capital stock by only about 0.5% from what it would otherwise have been.

How much pressure has this placed on wages in advanced countries? A reduction of the capital stock by 1% reduces productivity by less than 1%, since capital is only one input; standard estimates put the number at about 0.3%. A back-of-the-envelope calculation therefore suggests that capital flows to the Third World since 1990 (and bear in mind that there was essentially no capital flow during the 1980s) have reduced real wages in the advanced world by about 0.15%—hardly the devastation that Schwab, Delors, or the Economic Policy Institute presume.

There is another way to make the same point. Anything that draws capital away from business investment in the advanced countries tends to reduce First World wages. But investment in the Third World has become considerable only in the last few years. Meanwhile, there has been a massive diversion of savings into a purely domestic sink: the budget deficits run up by the United States and other countries. Since 1980, the United States alone has run up more than $3 trillion in federal debt, more than ten times the amount invested in emerging economies by all advanced countries combined. The export of capital to the Third World attracts a lot of attention because it is exotic, but the amounts are minor compared with domestic budget deficits.

At this point, some readers may object that one cannot compare the two numbers. Savings absorbed by the federal budget deficit simply disappear; savings invested abroad create factories that make products that then compete with ours. It seems plausible that overseas investment is more damaging than budget deficits. But that intuition is wrong: investing in Third World countries raises their productivity, and we've seen in the first two models that higher Third World productivity per se is unlikely to lower First World living standards.

The conventional wisdom among many policymakers and pundits is that we live in a world of incredibly mobile capital and that such mobility changes everything. But capital isn't all that mobile, and the capital movements we have seen so far change very little, at least for advanced countries.

Model 4: The Distribution of Income

We seem to have concluded that growth in the Third World has almost no adverse effects on the First World. But there is still one more issue to address: the effects of Third World growth on the distribution of income between skilled and unskilled labor within the advanced world.

For our final model, let's add one more complication. Suppose that there are two kinds of labor, skilled and unskilled. And suppose that the ratio of unskilled to skilled workers is much higher in the South than in the North. In such a situation, one would expect the ratio of skilled to unskilled wages to be lower in the North than in the South. As a result, one would expect the North to export skill-intensive goods and services— that is, employ a high ratio of skilled to unskilled labor in their production, while the South exports goods whose production is intensive in unskilled labor.

What is the effect of this trade on wages in the North? When two countries exchange skill-intensive goods for labor-intensive goods, they indirectly trade skilled for unskilled labor; the goods that the North ships to the South "embody" more skilled labor than the goods the North receives in return. It is as if some of the North's skilled workers migrated to the South. Similarly, the North's imports of labor-intensive products are like an indirect form of low-skill immigration. Trade with the South in effect makes Northern skilled labor scarcer, raising the wage it can command, while it makes unskilled labor effectively more abundant, reducing its wage.

Increased trade with the Third World, then, while it may have little effect on the overall level of First World wages, should in principle lead to greater *inequality* in those wages, with a higher premium for skill. Equally, there should be a tendency toward "factor price equalization," with wages of low-skilled workers in the North declining toward Southern levels.

What makes this conclusion worrisome is that income inequality has been rapidly increasing in the United States and to a lesser extent in other advanced nations. Even if Third World exports have not hurt the average level of wages in the First World, might they not be responsible for the steep declines since the 1970s in real wages of unskilled workers in the United States and the rising unemployment rates of European workers?

At this point, the preponderance of the evidence seems to be that factor price equalization has *not* been a major element in the growing wage inequality in the United States, although the evidence is more indirect and less secure than the evidence we brought to our earlier models.[2] In essence, trade with the Third World is just not that large. Since trade with low-wage countries is only a little more than 1% of GDP, the net flows of labor embodied in that trade are fairly small compared with the overall size of the labor force.

More careful research may lead to larger estimates of the effect of North-South trade on the distribution of wages, or future growth in that trade may have larger effects than we have seen so far. At this point, however, the available evidence does not support the view that trade with the Third World is an important part of the wage inequality story.

Moreover, even to the extent that North-South trade may explain some of the growing inequality of earnings, it has nothing to do with the disappointing performance of *average* wages. Before 1973, average compensation in the United States rose at an annual rate of more than 2%; since then it has risen at a rate of only 0.3%. This decline is at the heart of our economic malaise, and Third World exports have nothing to do with it.

The Real Threat

The view that competition from the Third World is a major problem for advanced countries is questionable in theory and flatly rejected by the data. Why does this matter? Isn't this merely academic quibbling? One answer is that those who talk about the dangers of competition with the Third World certainly think that it matters; the European Commission presumably did not add its comments about low-wage competition to its White Paper simply to fill space. If policymakers and intellectuals think it is important to emphasize the adverse effects of low-wage competition, then it is at least equally important for economists and business leaders to tell them they are wrong.

Ideas matter. According to recent newspaper reports, the United States and France have agreed to place demands for international standards on wages and working conditions on the agenda at the next GATT negotiations. U.S. officials will doubtless claim they have the interests of Third World workers at heart. Developing countries are already warning, however, that such standards are simply an effort to deny them access to world markets by preventing them from making use of the only competitive advantage they have: abundant labor. The developing countries are right. This is protectionism in the guise of humanitarian concern.

Most worrisome of all is the prospect that disguised protectionism will eventually give way to cruder, more open trade barriers. For example, Robert Kuttner has long argued that all world trade should be run along the lines of the Multi-Fiber Agreement, which fixes market shares for textile and apparel. In effect, he wants the cartelization of all world markets. Proposals like that are still outside the range of serious policy discussion, but when respectable voices lend credence to the wholly implausible idea that the Third World is responsible for the First World's problems, they prepare the way for that kind of heavy-handed interference in world trade.

We are not talking about narrow economic issues. If the West throws up barriers to imports out of a misguided belief that they will protect Western living standards, the effect could be to destroy the most promising aspect of today's world economy: the beginning of widespread economic development, of hopes for a decent living standard for hundreds of millions, even billions, of human beings. Economic growth in the Third World is an opportunity, not a threat; it is our fear of Third

World success, not that success itself, that is the real danger to the world economy.

Notes

1. The essential readings are J. R. Hicks on the long-run dollar problem in "An Inaugural Lecture," *Oxford Economic Papers* (New Series), June 1953; and H. G. Johnson, "Economic Expansion and International Trade," *Manchester School of Economic and Social Studies*, May 1995.

2. See Lawrence F. Katz, "Understanding Recent Changes in the Wage Structure," *NBER Reporter*, Winter 1992–93; and Robert Lawrence and Matthew Slaughter, "International Trade and American Wages in the 1980s: Giant Sucking Sound or Small Hiccup?" *Brookings Papers on Economic Activity* 2, 1993.

5   The Illusion of
        Conflict in
        International Trade

In the summer of 1993 the managing editor of *Foreign Affairs*—
a very intelligent, well-educated individual for whom I have a
great deal of respect—made a remark that only a few months
before would have startled me. I had proposed an article about
international economic relations, the article that was later to
become "Competitiveness: A Dangerous Obsession" (published
in *Foreign Affairs* the next March). And he said: "The conventional wisdom is that the military competition of the Cold War
has now been replaced by economic competition among the
market economies. Are you going to challenge that view?"

What was so startling about that remark? Well, to a trained
economist, the idea that international trade is a competition
that bears any serious resemblance to military rivalry sounds
very strange. Admittedly, there are many discussions of trade
conflict and sophisticated concepts of "strategic trade policy;"
but all efforts to actually put numbers to these issues reach the
conclusion that the stakes involved are very small, on the order
of a few tenths of one percent of national income—certainly
nothing like the life-and-death stakes involved in military
competition.

Reprinted by permission from *Peace Economics, Peace Science, and Public Policy*
(Winter 1995): 9–18.

So how could it be that an analogy between international trade and the Cold War could be described as the "conventional wisdom"? In this paper I want to offer three observations inspired by that question.

First, my editor was not ill-informed: the view of trade as a quasi-military competition is indeed the conventional wisdom among policymakers, business leaders, and influential intellectuals—that is, among the people who matter. It's not just that economists have lost control of the discourse; the kinds of ideas that are offered in a standard economics textbook do not enter into that discourse at all.

Second, the rejection of the conventional economic wisdom about the generally benign nature of international trade is not, as one might suppose, based on a justified skepticism about the realism of standard economic models. On the contrary, one gets nowhere in making sense of the debate on international "competitiveness," among people who regard themselves and are regarded by others as sophisticated, unless one realizes that their views are based on a failure to understand even the simplest economic facts and concepts.

Finally, because most of the discussion of international trade issues among those who matter is marked by deep ignorance—all the deeper because it often poses as sophistication—one must understand the risks of international economic confrontation as arising not from real conflicts of interest among nations, but from shadows and mirages. It is the illusion of economic conflict, which bears virtually no resemblance to the reality, that poses the real threat.

1   A Reading List

Perhaps the best way to illustrate the current state of discourse on international economics is to imagine the position of an intellectually-minded American—someone who watches McNeil-Lehrer, who reads *The Atlantic*, *The New Republic*, and *The New York Review of Books*, but is not a trained economist and not anxious to become one—who decides to educate himself or herself about the world economy. The natural thing to do would, of course, be to assemble a reading list of books that have been well-reviewed, by people whose names are familiar and whose faces he or she has seen on public television. What would such a reading list contain?

Well, here's a sample list:

(1) *Head to Head: The Coming Battle Among America, Japan, and Europe* by Lester Thurow: This book was, of course, a huge bestseller; it has also received respectful attention and endorsements from many influential people from President Clinton on down.

(2) *The Work of Nations* by Robert Reich: While not quite as large a seller as *Head to Head*, this book received many rapturous reviews; and Reich is, of course, not only Secretary of Labor but a key adviser to the President.

(3) *A Cold Peace: America, Japan, Germany and the Struggle for Supremacy* by Jeffrey Garten: Not a best-seller, but a book that has been praised by many powerful people; and on the strength of that book Garten was named to the key position of Undersecretary of Commerce for International Trade.

(4) *Trading Places* by Clyde Prestowitz: Prestowitz is a former trade official who now heads the Economic Strategy Institute, a very influential think tank; this book on how Japan has outwitted the United States received wide attention. Prestowitz is frequently quoted by leading columnists, and is a familiar face on television and in Congressional hearings.

(5) *The Endangered American Dream* by Edward Luttwak: Luttwak's reputation rests on his writings on politics and military

affairs, but this new tract on "geo-economics", which explicitly applies the parallel with strategic competition to international trade, attracted a great deal of notice.

(6) *The Silent War* by Ira Magaziner and Mark Patinkin: This book was not a mass seller, but it was well received among liberal leaders, and helped to cement Magaziner's reputation as a policy guru, which led to his role as architect of the Clinton health plan.

(7) *The World Competitiveness Report 1994*: The annual competitiveness reports by the World Economic Forum (which hosts the famous Davos conferences) invariably attract much favorable press attention. This latest report offers a grim assessment of the competitive pressures facing Western nations.

It's an impressive lineup: all of the authors of these books are men of very considerable influence and visibility. What do their books have in common?

One thing they have in common is a view of the world economy as a place of difficult struggle: a struggle for markets, for capital, in which countries that do not play the game as well as the world leaders are going to be in deep trouble. The books differ somewhat in how they describe the competition—for example, Reich portrays it largely as a struggle to attract a highly mobile pool of capital, while Thurow seems more concerned with a list of strategic industries. They also differ in their policy emphasis: Reich wants education and training, Thurow wants industrial policy, Prestowitz wants a tougher trade policy. But the theme of struggle, of "win-lose" competition, is common to all. Indeed, military metaphors abound; the martial tone is there in the titles or subtitles of Thurow, Garten, and Magaziner, and equally explicit in Luttwak's text.

The other thing these books have in common is a complete absence of anything that looks like the kind of international trade theory that academic economists teach. I don't mean that these authors challenge the economist's view. I mean that they write as if it does not exist.

It is important to be clear about the completeness with which academic economics is ignored. It is not a matter of a lack of familiarity with the latest wrinkles in research. Rather, *nothing* of international trade theory as economists know it— from Ricardo on—is in these books. Indeed, only Luttwak's book even mentions Ricardo or the concept of comparative advantage (the words occur in some of the other books, but used in a way that makes "comparative advantage" synonymous with "competitive advantage"); he grants Ricardo two sentences before dismissing the whole concept as irrelevant. The frameworks that are used to discuss international trade are either the author's own inventions, or, more often, derived from business and military strategy.

In other words, as far as the public discussion of international trade is concerned, economic analysis as it is done in the universities might as well not exist.

Surely, the reader must be about to argue, this goes too far. Aren't we making too much of a few authors? Don't economists have much more influence with the people who really matter?

Well, consider first just how impressive this author list is. Three of the authors are or were top officials in the Clinton Administration, and Thurow is arguably the world's best-known economist—certainly the best-selling economist. And the World Economic Forum would be surprised to be dismissed as consisting of people who don't really matter.

Moreover, are there any influential books or authors who do not share this lack of interest in standard economic analysis? To my knowledge, there has been no best-selling American book on economics in the past decade that made any reference at all to the conventional analysis of international trade—not even a hostile one.

Or perhaps we should not call the academic view "conventional." If by the conventional wisdom we mean the view that most important people hold, the view that people repeat to each other because they read it in the newspapers, and the view which the newspapers print because so many people repeat it, then the vision of international trade as a competition with winners and losers, a competition America had better win, *is* the conventional wisdom. The stuff that is in the college textbooks is a contrarian view, with hardly any real influence.

2 Who Is Right?

To many people who think and write about economics, the state that I have just described seems entirely appropriate. They view economics as, in John Kenneth Galbraith's words, "a failed profession," and regard indifference to what the professors have to say as precisely the right attitude. An acute observer should simply look at the world economy with fresh eyes, unencumbered by preconceptions derived from failed theories. If these authors ignore economic theory, it is because they know better.

I will come back to the question of why economists are so disdained later in this paper. For now, however, I want to focus on the question of whether the sort of international economic analysis that one finds in the reading list above is really better for its autonomy from any academic influence.

I can't, of course, do a detailed critique of every idea in all of these books. So let me focus on a particular theme that appears in several of them (Reich, Luttwak, the World Competitiveness Report): the threat posed to Western economies by competition from low-wage nations.

The *World Competitiveness Report* puts that threat starkly: "Today, the so-called industrialized nations employ 350 million people who are paid an average hourly wage of $18. However, during the past ten years, the world economy gained access to large and populated countries, such as China, the former Soviet Union, India, Mexico, etc. Altogether, it can be estimated that a labour force of some 1,200 million people has thus become reachable, at an average hourly cost of $2, and in many regions, under $1....

"[This] serves to demonstrate the massive pressure that exists today on labour in industrialized nations when a significant productivity advantage is not maintained. There is no doubt that many industries will be tempted to relocate in countries with low-cost labour. In a GATT world, where the right to operate in any country is guaranteed, and where the flow of goods, services, and capital investment is ensured, there is nothing to prevent companies from fully exploiting the respective comparative advantages of different countries on a global scale....

"As a result of this formidable specialization of world markets, the 'raison d'être' of many countries is at stake.... [An] outflow of manufacturing from Western economies seems inevitable.... Thus, the question of wealth creation in industrialized nations becomes more and more acute."

This offers a clear and compelling vision. Low-wage nations are now able to attract capital and technology from the advanced world. As a result, they can achieve productivity close to Western levels, while paying much lower wages. The result seems obvious: the low-wage countries will run huge trade surpluses, creating either large-scale unemployment or sharply falling wages in the erstwhile high-wage nations.

Sounds persuasive, doesn't it? There's only one problem: it is a vision that quite literally makes no sense.

The reason lies in a basic fact of accounting, perhaps the most essential equation in international economics:

Savings − Investment = Exports − Imports

This is not a hypothetical theory: it is an unavoidable accounting identity, a statement of an adding-up constraint that any consistent story about any economy must honor. And yet it is an equation that the story in the *World Competitiveness Report* clearly violates.

Consider that story again. It asserts that capital will move from Western nations to low-wage countries—that is, that those nations will be able to invest more than their domestic savings because foreign capital will also be investing there. So for these economies the left-hand side of the equation is negative: investment exceeds savings. At the same time, it asserts that low-wage countries will export much more than they import, "deindustrializing" the advanced nations. So the right hand side is... positive?

When I have tried to explain this problem to people who find the story about low-wage competition persuasive, their first reaction is to ask what alternative story I propose. The obvious answer is that as capital and technology flow to low-wage nations, their wage rates will rise along with their productivity. As a result they will not run huge trade surpluses with advanced nations, indeed, they will run deficits, as the counterpart to the capital inflows. The usual reaction to this is that it is implausible, and that it is a typical economist's assertion that markets will always do the right thing. I then ask what the questioner proposes; he replies that he believes that low-wage countries will run big trade surpluses. "So you think that low-wage countries are going to export large quantities of capital to high-wage nations?" At this point the conversation gets unpleasant, with some remark about this kind of thing being the reason why people hate economists.

It might also be worth noting that in these arguments people often bring in the observation that when multinational corporations have opened plants in low-wage countries, they often achieve near-First-World productivity but continue to pay Third World wages. The economist's answer to this is that it is exactly what one should expect: wage rates should reflect average national productivity, not productivity in a particular factory; if only a few modern factories have opened in a country, they will not raise that country's average productivity by much and should therefore not be expected to pay high wages. (And of course a country with low overall productivity that is able to achieve near-U.S. productivity in a few goods will tend to export those goods; it's called comparative advantage). But no matter how much one tries to explain that this outcome is exactly what the standard model predicts, it seems to be viewed as somehow a decisive rejection of the economist's optimism about the trade balance.

So what do we learn from this example? First, we learn that there are very simple things in economic theory—things that are not really debatable, like accounting identities, or very basic principles, like the idea that wages should reflect average national productivity rather than productivity at the plant level—which are very easy for people who have no familiarity with academic economics to get wrong. (And stories that embody these confusions can seem so much more persuasive than stories that are internally consistent that people will cling to them doggedly, even angrily, in the teeth of the arithmetic). In other words, economists do seem to know something worthwhile.

And second, we learn that the authors of the books on my reading list do not base their disdain for academic economics on a superior or more subtle understanding. Rather, their views are startlingly crude and uninformed. I have actually made the case only for the low-wage competition argument, which figures prominently in only some of the books. However, all of the authors on my reading list, both in these books and in their other writings, display an astonishing range of errors and misconceptions—errors of fact, mangled statistics, supposedly sophisticated arguments based on double-counting, failures to understand basic ideas about competition. (If you think that I am overstating the case, look at the exchange in the July/August 1994 issue of *Foreign Affairs*).

It seems, then, that I am asserting that the conventional wisdom about international trade is dominated by entirely ignorant men, who have managed to convince themselves and everyone else who matters that they have deep insights, but are in fact unaware of the most basic principles of and facts about the world economy; and that the disdained academic economists are at least by comparison fonts of wisdom and common sense. And that is indeed my claim. But then two questions arise: How has this state of affairs come to pass? And does it matter?

3 The Anatomy of Anti-economics

As far as I can tell, the attitude of policy-minded intellectuals to economics is pretty much unique. Many people have opinions about legal matters or about defense policy; but they generally accept that a fair amount of specialized knowledge is necessary to discuss these matters intelligently. Thus a law degree is expected of a commentator on legal affairs, a professional military career or a record of study of military matters is expected of a commentator on defense, and so on.

When it comes to economics, however, and especially international trade, it seems to be generally accepted that there is
no specialized knowledge to master. Lawyers, political scien-
tists, historians cheerfully offer their views on the subject, and
often seem quite sure that whatever it is that the professors
have to say—something they are fairly blurry about—is naive
and wrong.

Let me offer a revealing quotation, from another well-known
author: Professor Paul Kennedy, author of *The Rise and Fall of
the Great Powers* and *Preparing for the 21st Century*. Professor
Kennedy is a historian by training, but lately he has taken to
writing and speaking about international economics. Here is
what he said in the *New Perspectives Quarterly*: "Granted, again,
that modernization is unstoppable, how does it work when
production of an item takes place not just in a specific region
like western Europe in the 19th century or East Asia in the late
20th century, but *globally* ... when there are 50 countries, with
varying standards of wages, capable of producing soybeans,
and 70 countries capable of producing steel? Adam Smith's
argument in favor of free trade and specialization, that it made
no economic sense for both England and Portugal to strive to
produce wine and textiles when England's climate made it a
better textile producer and Portugal's climate made it a better
wine producer, doesn't address this reality of *multiple*, competitive sources—yet it is the basis of modern, free-market economics. What if there is *nothing* you can produce more cheaply
or efficiently than elsewhere, except by constantly cutting labor costs?"

Many readers of this article will be people who have some
interest in international economics, without necessarily being
trained economists, and consider themselves reasonably well-
informed about the subject. For these readers, the key question

is: did you find the quotation from Professor Kennedy hysteri-
cally funny?

If not, shame on you. First of all, Kennedy confuses David
Ricardo with Adam Smith. This may sound like a petty point.
But suppose that an intellectual were to offer what he thought
was a deep critique of psychoanalysis—a field considerably
less well-grounded in evidence and logic than international
trade theory—and immediately begin by showing that he did
not know the difference between Freud and Jung? Or suppose
that a critic of evolution were not to know the difference
between Darwin and Mendel?

More important, however, is the way that Kennedy feels
that he is in a position to discuss the idea of comparative
advantage—"the basis of modern, free-market economics"—
without understanding the idea. Kennedy's concern that your
country may have nothing it can produce more efficiently than
anyone else is the classic fallacy of confusing *comparative* advantage with *absolute* advantage. (It's a fallacy discussed on
page 20 of the best-selling undergraduate textbook). Again, it's
as if someone dismissed Freud for claiming that everyone con-
sciously wants to marry his mother and kill his father.

While this quotation is unusually revealing, the attitude
it displays—that international economics requires no special
knowledge, and that the theories of the academics, whatever
they are, are obviously silly—is extremely common. Indeed,
the author of one of the books on my reading list smugly
assured me that if you wanted to be taken seriously as an
economic commentator an academic training was a liability.

But why is this attitude so prevalent? At this point I am in
the awkward position of having to defend economic profes-
sionalism by playing amateur sociologist, but let me offer the
following five-part hypothesis.

First, economics is a subject that touches so many real-world concerns that there is a great incentive to claim expertise. This is especially true of international economics, in which the romance and allure of anything to which the word "global" is attached adds to the attraction of the enterprise. As a result, a large number of people inevitably propound views about international economics without much background in the subject.

Second, ignorance finds strength in numbers. Since so many lawyers, political experts, etc. feel free to opine on economics, others considering such a role do not hesitate over their lack of formal qualifications or knowledge of the field.

Third, economics written by non-economists often sounds more persuasive than the real thing. This is not just a matter of jargon: no matter how well explained, serious economic analysis is often intrinsically difficult. Did you understand why low-wage countries cannot both run trade surpluses and attract capital inflows on the first reading? (Do you understand it now?)

Fourth, there is a lot of bad-mouthing of economists. This is understandable. After all, suppose you are, say, a military expert who has decided that he is an economic expert too. You write an article or even a book on the subject; then an academic economist tells you that all of your ingenious arguments are familiar fallacies covered in an undergraduate textbook, and that your basic thesis involves a contradiction because you do not understand national accounts. You might decide that you really should go back and read a basic textbook; more likely, you begin denigrating economists as pompous types who actually don't know anything.

And finally, the bad-mouthing of economists, by people who typically have rapport with their audience because they share that audience's misconceptions, reinforces the perception that economists have nothing to offer—which encourages more non-economists to declare themselves experts, enter the fray, and reinforces the cycle.

In short, there is a circular process by which bad ideas drive out good. As far as the public discourse on international trade is concerned, this process is essentially complete: not only sophisticated theories, but comparative advantage and even $S - I = X - M$ have been driven out of the discussion.

And that means that if you want to understand the potential for economic conflict among the major nations, you need to understand that these countries' policies are unlikely to be based on anything resembling an accurate perception of their national interest. On the contrary: they will be informed by a view of trade as conflict that dissolves at the first serious confrontation with logic or evidence.

4 Does It Matter?

At the time of writing, the U.S. Congress had just passed the legislation implementing the latest GATT round, and committing the United States to joining the new World Trade Organization. A year previously the same Congress approved the North American Free Trade Agreement. Although the Clinton Administration made a lot of noise in its negotiations with Japan, at least as of the end of 1994 no trade war had broken out or seemed likely to break out anytime soon. So despite the ignorance about international economics displayed by authors who became top Clinton officials, the actual performance of the Administration has been quite gratifying to a free trader. What damage, then, does the illusion of conflict that pervades intellectual discussion actually do?

One answer, which I would argue quite strongly, involves what we might call collateral damage. The authors of these books made their reputations by expressing ideas about the international economy that their readers perceived as wise and deep. On the strength of their ideas their advice was solicited, they were given high-level government jobs, put in charge of crucial task forces. But not only weren't their ideas wise and deep: they were inexcusably wrong, wrong in a way that should have been obvious to anyone who knew a little basic economics and was willing to spend an hour or so in the reference section of a college library. Might one then not worry about the kind of advice these men might give and the kind of decisions they might take?

But there is a concern which bears more directly on international trade. It is true that most of the authors I have cited are not outright protectionists. But it is hard to see why. If you take the economic arguments in the *World Competitiveness Report* seriously, they point quite clearly to the desirability of shutting off trade and capital movement between high- and low-wage countries. The authors refuse to draw that conclusion—but their attempts to avoid it are transparently stuck onto the end of an argument that is clearly pointing the other way. The same may be said of the other books. What seems to be happening is that the idea of being an outright protectionist is still unacceptable in polite company; so whatever each author's argument, he always ends up with some more respectable recommendation, such as training or limited industrial policy.

It is hard to imagine, however, that free trade can long survive as the official ideology of policy intellectuals when the real arguments in its favor have been effectively driven out of the public discourse. There is a book which I did not put on my reading list, but which has already been the top-selling book in France. In its economic argument it is essentially identical to the *World Competitiveness Report*, but it does not suffer from that report's lingering concerns over the unacceptability of frank protectionism.

The book is *The Trap*, by James Goldsmith. It is a terrible book; its economic argument is nothing but the classic "pauper labor" fallacy (page 21 of the textbook), mixed in with a thorough ignorance of basic facts. But it has one virtue: the courage of its convictions. And Sir James's willingness to take the rhetoric of international conflict to its logical conclusion, to espouse frank protectionism—Goldsmith basically believes that trade should only be allowed between countries at similar wage levels—have been exactly what the educated French public wanted. (It remains to be seen how the book does in English translation).

I believe that if the rhetoric that portrays international trade as a struggle continues to dominate the discourse, then policy debate will in the end be dominated by men like Goldsmith, who are willing to take that rhetoric to its logical conclusion. That is, trade will be treated as war, and the current system of relatively open world markets will disintegrate because nobody but a few professors believes in the ideology of free trade.

And that will be a shame, because for all their faults the professors are right. The conflict among nations that so many policy intellectuals imagine prevails is an illusion; but it is an illusion that can destroy the reality of mutual gains from trade.

II

Economic Theory,
Good and Bad

6   Myths and Realities of U.S. Competitiveness

A generation ago, international trade was largely ignored by the U.S. public. Today, however, concern about international competitiveness pops up in virtually every policy discussion— whether the subject is education, the budget deficit, or pollution control. Unpopular measures are defended on the grounds that they will make our economy more competitive, and popular initiatives are opposed because they are alleged to threaten our competitive position.

The roots of public concern over the competitive position of the United States are obvious. International trade has become increasingly important to the U.S. economy: imports are three times as high a share of national income as they were a generation ago. At the same time, U.S. economic pre-eminence in the world has visibly declined: U.S. national income, once larger than that of the rest of the world's market economics combined, is now less than 30% of the total; U.S. leadership in advanced technology, once nearly total, has been challenged in a variety of areas; what was once an overwhelming U.S. productivity advantage over other industrial countries has given

Reprinted by permission from *Science* (November 8, 1991): 811–815. © 1991 by the American Association for the Advancement of Science.

way to a rough parity, at least in manufacturing, with clear U.S. inferiority in some sectors.

In spite of nearly universal concerns over competitiveness, however, there is surprisingly little coherent discussion of what "competitiveness" means. It is probably fair to say that most people who use the term think of a country as being like a business and of international trade as being like business competition writ large. In the business world, of course, competitiveness has a clear meaning: a firm that is uncompetitive—that is, which fails to offer a product as good as its rivals, or to keep its cost low enough—will lose market share and eventually go out of business. In fact, however, a country is not much like a business. Indeed, trade between countries is so much unlike competition between business that many economists regard the word "competitiveness," when applied to countries, as so misleading as to be essentially meaningless.

Yet people who worry about U.S. competitiveness are not inventing their concerns our of thin air. They are responding to a perception that the United States has actually been losing something important in the process of international competition. And while the crude view that sees a country as being just like a business is wrong, the view that failure to cope with international competition can sometimes be injurious to a country's economic health is right.

My purpose in this article, is to offer a clarification of the issue of international competitiveness. First, I attempt to dispel some "myths" about competitiveness—that is, some widely held ideas that grow out of the false analogy between a country and a business. Then, I turn to the "realities" of competitiveness—the sources of valid concern.

Myths of Competitiveness

The issue of competitiveness is often presented in apocalyptic terms: If America does not shape up to cope with international competition, it will face some kind of economic catastrophe. This extreme view grows out of a false analogy between nations and businesses. A useful way to point up what is wrong with this analogy is by a simple thought experiment.

Imagine first a world in which labor productivity around the world grows at an annual rate of 1%, both in the United States and abroad. It would seem reasonable to suppose in that case that living standards, real wages, and so on would rise by about 1% per year everywhere.

Now suppose that U.S. productivity were to continue its 1% growth rate, but that productivity growth in other countries were to accelerate, say to 4% annually. What would happen to the welfare of U.S. residents as a result?

To many people it would seem obvious that the United States would be in serious trouble. After all, a firm whose productivity lags behind its rivals will find itself losing markets, forced to lay off workers, and eventually driven our of business. Won't the same happen to a nation?

The answer is "No." International competition does not put countries out of business. There are strong equilibrating forces that normally ensure that any country remains able to sell a range of goods in world markets, and to balance its trade on average over the long run, even if its productivity, technology, and product quality are inferior to those of other nations. And even countries that are clearly inferior in productivity to their trading partners are normally made better, not worse, off by international trade.

The classic analysis of the equilibrating forces in international trade is more than two centuries old. David Hume (1), living in a world in which precious metals were still the principal medium of exchange, pointed out that a country that had for some reason become uncompetitive, and as a result was importing more than it exported, would suffer a steady drain of gold and silver coins. This fall in the money supply, however, would lead to a fall in the level of prices and wages in that country; eventually goods and labor would become sufficiently cheap in the deficit nation that its goods would again become attractive to buyers, and the trade deficit would be corrected.

In the modern world the adjustment process is more complex and less automatic. In a world of national currencies no longer backed by gold, deficit countries usually adjust by depreciating their currencies rather than by letting wages and prices fall. Also, international capital movements have as their counterpart trade imbalances: A country that is able to attract an inflow of foreign capital will (as a matter of sheer accounting identity) also run a trade deficit, whereas a country that is exporting capital will run a surplus. Nonetheless, over the long term, major industrial countries show a strong tendency toward equality of imports and exports, regardless of their productivity and technological performance. Table 6.1 shows the balance on current account (a broad definition of trade in goods and services) of the three major industrial countries as a per-

Table 6.1
Long-run self-correction of payments imbalances (10). Figures for 1991 are estimated.

Country	Current account balances (% of GNP)		
	1960–88	1987	1991
United States	−0.2	−3.6	−1.7
Japan	1.0	3.6	1.8
Germany	1.1	4.1	2.3

centage of their national incomes for selected time periods. The average imbalances over the long term are quite small. During the mid-1980s large imbalances emerged, attributed by many economists to the unprecedented U.S. budget deficit and other special factors. By early 1991 about half of this divergence had again been eliminated (due in large part to a sharp rise of the dollar value of the yen and the mark), and the United States in particular was experiencing a broad-based export recovery.

Suppose that a country lags behind other nations in productivity. The equilibrating forces first noticed by Hume ensure that it will nonetheless be able to find a range of goods and services to export. But what will it export? The answer, pointed out by David Ricardo (2) in 1817, is that a country whose productivity lags that of its trading partners in all or almost all industries will export those goods in which its productivity disadvantage is smallest. In the standard terminology of international economics, a country will always find a range of goods in which it has a "comparative advantage" even if there are no goods in which it has an "absolute advantage."

The classic empirical example of the principle of comparative advantage at work comes from the early post-war comparison of Britain and the United States (3). At that time, British productivity was far less than that of the United States—labor productivity in manufacturing was below U.S. levels in all major industries, and on average was less than half of the United States. The British economy, however, was much more dependent on foreign trade, and therefore was obliged to generate approximately the same dollar value of export earnings. If one looks at the comparative pattern of exports, one seems a clear picture of comparative advantage at work. Figure 6.1, plotted from data for a set of 22 industries, shows that there is a clear-cut association between relative productivity and relative exports. U.S. productivity was higher in all cases; but only in

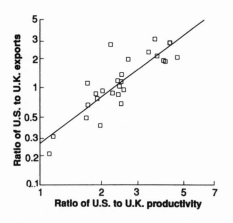

Figure 6.1
Relations between U.S. and U.K. productivity and exports, 1950–1951 (13).

industries in which U.S. productivity was more than about 2.5 times U.K. productivity did the United States have larger exports. That is, Britain did not have an absolute advantage in anything, but it had a comparative advantage in those goods in which its productivity exceeded 40% of the U.S. level.

Britain's ability to outsell the United States in industries in which its productivity was inferior depended, of course, on the fact that British workers were paid less than U.S. workers—a pay differential that was greatly widened by the 1949 devaluation of the pound from $4.80 to $2.80. A common reaction to this observation, and to such events as the recovery of U.S. exports that followed the decline in the dollar between 1985 and 1988, is that coping with international competition by lowering relative wages must lower a country's living standards. Ricardo's 1817 discussion of comparative advantage showed, however, that trade between two nations ordinarily raises the standard of living of both, even if one must compete on the basis of low wages.

We may see this point with a hypothetical example, similar to one introduced by Ricardo. Imagine a world in which the United States and Britain are the only trading countries and that there are only two goods, wool and aircraft. Suppose also that labor is the only input into production, and that U.S. labor is more productive than British in both. The U.S. advantage is, however, much more pronounced in aircraft. Table 6.2 illustrates a hypothetical set of productivity numbers.

Clearly, if these two countries are going to be able to sell goods to each other, the U.S. wage rate must be at least 1.5 times that of Britain—otherwise both goods would be cheaper to produce in America—but no more than 6 times as high. The actual wage rate would depend on demand conditions and the relative size of the economies, but let us simply suppose that the relative wage rate is 3. At that wage rate, wool would be cheaper to produce in Britain, which would therefore export it, whereas aircraft would be cheaper to produce in the United States. If prices are proportional to labor cost, one unit of wool, which requires one-half unit of British labor, would trade for one unit of aircraft, which requires one-sixth unit of the more expensive U.S. labor.

Now we ask, "Is Britain better or worse off trading with the United States, on the basis of a wage rate only one-third as high, than it would be in the absence of trade?" The answer is that it is better off. In the absence of trade, it would take one

Table 6.2
Gains from trade in spite of lagging productivity.

| Country | Hypothetical productivity numbers | |
	Aircraft	Wool
United States	6	3
United Kingdom	1	2

unit of British labor to produce one unit of aircraft. By trading with America, Britain can acquire an aircraft by trading a unit of wool for it, which requires the use of only one-half unit of labor. That is, the opportunity to trade with America raises the purchasing power of British labor (4).

This is a grossly simplified example, but it makes a crucial point. A country that is less productive than its trading partners across the board will be forced to compete on the basis of low wages rather than superior productivity. But it will not suffer catastrophe, and indeed will normally still benefit from international trade. The point is that international trade, unlike competition among businesses for a limited market, is not a zero-sum game in which one nation's gain is another's loss. It is positive-sum game, which is why the word "competitiveness" can be dangerously misleading when applied to international trade.

Although this is a crucial point to appreciate, it is also important to understand what the example has and has not demonstrated. Returning to our thought experiment, we have not shown that the United States, with its 1% annual productivity growth, is as well off as it would be if it shared the rest of the world's 4% growth; clearly, it is not. Nor have we even shown that the United States is better off with the rest of the world growing at 4% than at 1%. In fact, it could be either better or worse off; this depends on details, specifically on whether rest-of-world growth is biased toward goods the U.S. exports (in which case the United States is hurt) or toward goods that the United States imports (in which case the United States is helped) (5). All that we have shown is that low productivity does not pose a worse problem for a country that is engaged in international trade than for one that is not. Britain in 1950 had a productivity problem (and still does); the negative impact of that problem on Britain's standard of living, however, was no greater, and in fact less, because Britain was a trading nation rather than a self-sufficient society.

We should also note that the discussion here has so far omitted a factor that is critical in the real-world politics of international trade: income distribution. Changes in international trading patterns often have strong effects on the distribution of income within countries, so that even a generally beneficial change produces losers as well as winners (at least in the short run). If foreigners are willing to sell us high-quality goods cheaply, that is a good thing for most of us, but a bad thing for the domestic industry that competes with the imports. This observation cuts both ways. On one side, economists sometimes blithely speak of the benefits of free trade, ignoring the sometimes substantial costs of adjustment. On the other hand, much opposition to free trade represents special interest pleading, and an appeal to the need for "competitiveness" is often used as a cloak for narrow self-interest.

Realities of Competitiveness

The discussion so far seems to suggest that competitiveness, if it means anything, is a non-issue: Even unproductive countries have a range of goods in which they have a comparative advantage, and more or less automatic forces will always ensure that a country is competitive in industries in which it has a comparative advantage. Yet we should not be too quick to dismiss the idea that there is some real problem to which concerns about competitiveness are a response. For in the discussion above I have made an implicit assumption that is clearly untrue in some instances—that countries' comparative advantages determine their pattern of trade, rather than the other way around.

Much international trade is driven by enduring national differences in resources, climate, and society. Brazil is a coffee exporter because of soil and climate, Saudi Arabia an oil exporter because of geology, Canada a wheat exporter because of the abundance of land relative to labor, and so on. Trade in manufactured goods among advanced industrial countries, however, particularly in higher sophisticated products, is harder to explain (6). In many cases industries seem to create their own comparative advantage, through a process of positive feedback.

The process through which comparative advantage can be created is illustrated in Fig. 6.2. Suppose that a country has for whatever reason established a strong presence in a particular industry. Then this presence may produce what in standard terminology are called "external economies" that reinforce the industry's strength. External economies come in two main variants. So-called technological external economies involve the spillover of knowledge between firms: to the extent that firms can learn from each other, a strong national industry can give rise to a national knowledge base that reinforces the industry's

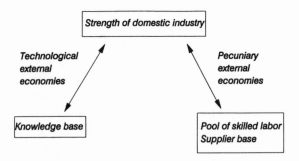

Figure 6.2
Self-reinforcing comparative advantage.

advantage. Pecuniary external economies depend on the size of the market: a strong domestic industry offers a large market for specialized labor and suppliers, and the availability of a flexible labor pool and an efficient supplier base reinforces the industry's strength.

When external economies are powerful, international specialization can have a strong arbitrary quality. During an industry's informative years, or during a transitional period when shifts in technology or markets have invalidated existing patterns of advantage, a country may establish a lead in an industry due to historical accident—or government support. Once this lead is established, it becomes self-reinforcing and tends to persist.

The importance of external economies is obvious in interregional specialization within the United States. Such famous industry clusters as Silicon Valley and Route 128, as well as less well-known examples like the cluster of carpet manufacturers around Dalton, Georgia (or the insurance cluster in Hartford, Connecticut) clearly reflect the self-reinforcing effects of success rather than underlying resources. International examples include Swiss watches, Italian ceramic tiles, and the role of London as a financial center.

It is probably true that external economies are a more important determinant of international trade in high-technology sectors than elsewhere, although they are by no means restricted to high tech. There is some dispute over whether the basis of international trade has shifted away from traditional comparative advantage toward created advantage. What is definitely true is that although the idea of external economies is an old one, going back to Marshall (7), recent developments in the analysis of international trade have placed increasing emphasis on the role of history, accident, and government policy in producing trade patterns (8).

The proposition that comparative advantage may be created rather than exogenously given somewhat qualifies the generally benign picture of international competition given in the first part of this paper. It suggests that under some circumstances countries may lose, or fail to establish, industries in which in the long run they might have been able to acquire a comparative advantage. This, in turn, provides a potential case for government intervention.

The traditional version of this line of reasoning is the infant industry argument for developing countries. Countries new to industrialization, the argument goes, face established competitors who already have the knowledge base, suppliers, and specialized skills in industries where these are important. Absent government intervention, the new entrants will therefore find themselves producing only goods in which external economies are unimportant, and will be stuck with permanently lower wages. By promoting targeted industries, they can in principle escape from this trap.

The new version of the argument involves established countries but new industries. Let us set up an exaggerated case, bearing in mind that it overstates the reality. Suppose that the United States trades with Japan and that Japan systematically promotes new high-technology industries as they emerge. This promotion may take the form of government subsidy, but it can also take the form of explicit or implicit protection of the domestic market, which both denies U.S. firms an important market and ensures Japanese firms of sales. Then, other things equal, Japan will tend to establish a competitive advantage in emerging high-technology sectors. This will not be catastrophic for the United States: the principle of comparative advantage still applies, and the United States will still find a range of goods to export. It will, however, increasingly be forced to compete on the basis of low wages rather than high productivity.

Table 6.3
Evidence of the closed Japanese market for high technology is shown by the figures for the domestic share of the home market for high-technology goods (11).

Year	Domestic share (%)		
	Germany	Japan	United States
1970	77	94	95
1980	59	93	89
1985	43	94	84

This story bears enough resemblance to reality to touch some raw nerves. Japan does not engage in extensive subsidy to industry, and on paper its markets are quite open to imports of manufactured goods. In practice, however, as indicated in Table 6.3, the Japanese market for high-technology goods has remained a virtually closed preserve for Japanese firms, whereas such markets have become increasingly internationalized not only in the United States but also in Europe.

This, then, is the real competitiveness issue: The possibility that international competition will exclude the United States from some industries in which it could or should have had a comparative advantage. Having identified this as a valid argument, we need to offer some strong warnings against overuse.

First, although government subsidy and unequal access to markets have surely played an important role in determining the outcome of international competition in a few industries, they are unlikely to be the major explanation of disappointing U.S. economic performance. Most of the output of U.S. economy is not traded internationally: in 1990, imports and exports were only 13 and 12.3% of gross national product, respectively. Furthermore, as Table 6.4 shows, since 1980 the United States has actually experienced a striking revival of productivity growth in manufacturing, which is precisely the sector most

Table 6.4
Comparisons of major industrial nations.

Country	Net national savings % of GNP, 1980−1988 (10)	National R&D % of GDP, 1987 (11)	Rate of growth of manufacturing productivity (12):	
			1970−1980	1980−1988
United States	3.6	1.8	2.3	3.7
Japan	17.8	2.8	6.4	5.5
West Germany	9.8	2.6	4.2	2.8

exposed to international competition. To the extent that the United States continues to perform poorly compare with other major industrial nations, this has a great deal to do with a low national savings rate, low spending on R&D, and low-quality basic education. Failure to create advantage is at best a contributing factor.

Second, the national pursuit of competitive advantage should not be unrestrained, because unilateral pursuit of advantage can work to everyone's disadvantage. For example, the United Kingdom undoubtedly derives significant benefits from the London's role as the financial capital of Europe, benefits that would be lost if that capital were in, say, Frankfurt instead. Yet Europe as a whole would almost surely be worse off if nationalistic policies led to a fragmented financial system divided among Frankfurt, Paris, Milan, and London. That is, it is better for the British that the City be in Britain rather than elsewhere; but it is in the common interest that there be a City (or a Silicon Valley or Route 128) somewhere, so that the advantages of such a cluster's external economies can be realized.

Finally, competitiveness is one of those issues, like national defense, that can easily be used as a patriotic cloak for special interest politics. The infant industry argument, mentioned above, is intellectually impeccable. In practice, however, it has been used in many developing countries to justify policies that maintain highly inefficient industries and generate large economic benefits for a politically influential elite (9). The risks of a similar misuse of intellectually legitimate concerns about U.S. competitiveness mean that arguments for a more nationalistic trade policy, while they should not be dismissed out of hand, need to be treated with caution.

Summary and Conclusions

There are valid reasons for concern over U.S. international competitiveness, but they are not what most people think. The common fear is that an economy that fails to keep up with its trading partners will suffer severe economic damage—incurable trade deficits, large-scale unemployment, perhaps economic collapse. This fear is unjustified. Both in theory and in practice, countries with lagging productivity are still able to balance their international trade, because what drives trade is comparative rather than absolute advantage. Maintaining productivity growth and technological progress is extremely important; but it is important for its own sake, not because it is necessary to keep up with international competition.

The real competitive issue is subtler. There is no question that in many cases comparative advantage arises from self-reinforcing external economies rather than as a result of underlying national resources. In such cases international competition may exclude a country from an industry in which it could have established a comparative advantage, or drive a country from an industry in which comparative advantage could have been maintained. In these cases, a intellectually respectable argument can be made for government policies to create or preserve advantage.

The fact that an argument is intellectually respectable does not mean that it is right. Concerns over competitiveness that are valid in principle can be and have been misused or abused in practice. Competitiveness is both a subtler and a more problematic issue than is generally understood.

References and Notes

1. D. Hume, *Writings on Economics* (Univ. of Wisconsin Press, Madison, 1955).

2. D. Ricardo, *The Principles of Political Economy and Taxation* (Irwin, Homewood, IL, 1963).

3. A similar relation between relative productivity and exports applies between the United States and Japan today. The U.S.–U.K. comparison from the early post-war period, however, remains a particularly revealing example, because Britain was able to export about as much as the United States in spite of an overwhelming U.S. productivity advantage across the board.

4. The converse is also true: the high-productivity, high-wage country also gains from trade. It is commonly argued that industrial countries are hurt by competition from low-wage nations using "sweatshop labor"; this is just as wrong as the argument that being a low-wage country is worse than not trading at all.

5. For analysis of the effects of foreign growth on domestic welfare, see H. Johnson, *Manch. Sch. Econ. Stud.* 23, 95 (1955). Any adverse effects would come through a worsening of the terms of trade, that is, the price of exports relative to that of imports. Excluding oil and agricultural goods, U.S. terms of trade have in fact shown a slight downward trend, but the trend is too small to have a significant negative effect on U.S. welfare [R. Lawrence, *Brookings Pap. Econ. Activity* 2: 1990, 343 (1990)].

6. Most trade in manufactured goods among industrial countries consist of "intra-industry" trade, that is, exchange of goods that seem to be produced using similar ratios of capital to labor and of skilled to unskilled workers. Thus it is difficult to explain the pattern of compar-

ative advantage among industrial countries by differences in their resource mixes, which are in any case quite similar [H. Grubel and P. Lloyd, *Intra-Industry Trade* (Wiley, New York, 1975); E. Helpman, *J. Jpn. Int. Econ.* 1, 62 (1987).

7. A. Marshall, *Principles of Economics* (Macmillan, London, 1920).

8. During the 1980s, the so-called "new international economics," which emphasized the arbitrary aspect of the international trade pattern, received wide academic acceptance. This is now a huge field; for surveys, see E. Helpman and P. Krugman, *Market Structure and Foreign Trade* (MIT Press, Cambridge, MA, 1985); P. Krugman, *Rethinking International Trade* (MIT Press, Cambridge, MA, 1990). In less academic contexts, M. Porter [*The Competitive Advantage of Nations* (Basic Books, New York, 1990) and B. Arthur [*Sci. Am.* 262, 92 (1990)] have made the case for the crucial role of external economies. I borrow the useful analogy with positive feedback from Arthur.

9. India provides a particularly good (which is to say bad) example of disastrous economic policies justified in the name of economic development. See the survey of Indian economics in *The Economist* (3–9 May 1991).

10. Organization for Economic Cooperation and Development, *Main Economic Indicators: Historical Statistics* (Paris, 1990); International Monetary Fund, *World Economic Outlook* (Washington, DC, October 1990).

11. National Science Board, *Science and Engineering Indicators 1989* (Washington, DC, 1990).

12. Bureau of Labor Statistics, *Handbook of Labor Statistics* (U.S. Government Printing Office, Washington, DC, 1990).

13. B. Balassa, *Rev. Econ. Stat.* 45, 231 (1963).

7 Economic Shuttle Diplomacy: A Review of Laura D'Andrea Tyson's *Who's Bashing Whom?*

Laura D'Andrea Tyson's selection as President Clinton's chief economic adviser has brought *Who's Bashing Whom?*, her book on international trade policy in high technology industries, widespread attention. The book deserves it: it's an impressive work, lucidly written, full of useful information, yet agreeably modest in its claims. Even before the author's new visibility, it had become must reading for anybody interested in trade policy and a rallying point for sophisticated critics of the traditional case for free trade.

And yet one wonders how many of the book's new readers will really understand the issues it raises. For one thing, in spite of the excellence of the writing, it's pretty heavy going even for professionals. The core of *Who's Bashing Whom* is a series of case studies, each of which tells you more than you probably want to know about a high-technology industry, leading up in each case to a highly qualified and equivocated set of conclusions. This density of argument is unavoidable, as I'll explain later; but my guess is that few people will actually read the book cover to cover.

More important, *Who's Bashing Whom* can't really be understood unless placed in context. Read in isolation, the book is like the middle of an argument. You don't get the point unless you know what came before and what comes after.

I

Tyson begins her book with a critique of the traditional case for free trade. In so doing, she presumes that her readers understand that case. Yet, in fact, very few people, even those who think themselves well-informed, do understand it. They tend to think of the defense of free trade as a kind of ideological prejudice, instead of the deep (if not unchallengeable) insight it really is. You can't make sense of Tyson's argument without appreciating the intellectual force of the tradition she wants to modify.

If there is a single slogan that sums up what economists have to say about trade, it is this: *A country is not like a corporation.* A corporation is essentially competing with its rivals over a limited pool of potential profits; it must be at least as good in some lines of business as those rivals or it will eventually fail. Countries, by contrast, don't go out of business, and international trade is much more a matter of (usually) mutually beneficial exchange than it is of competition and rivalry.

To understand why countries are not essentially in competition with each other, it is useful to imagine a simplified world in which there are only two countries—call them, arbitrarily, America and Mexico—and in which labor of uniform skill is the only productive resource. (Some readers will recognize this example as a variant on the one offered by David Ricardo more than 170 years ago.) To sharpen the case, let's also suppose that labor in America is more productive in every activity than labor in Mexico, but that the productivity differential varies across industries. For example, American labor may be 10 times as productive as Mexican in the manufacture of high-technology goods, but only 50 percent more productive in the manufacture of apparel.

What's going to happen if these countries begin to trade with each other? The answer obviously depends on the ratio of their wage rates. If the Mexican wage is too high, almost everything will be more cheaply produced by the more productive American workers. If, on the other hand, Mexican wages are low enough, most goods will be cheaper to produce in Mexico. But relative wage rates do not fall from the sky, they are determined in the marketplace. And they will therefore tend to settle somewhere in the middle, at a level at which each country has a range of goods that it can produce more cheaply. In the useful jargon of international trade theorists, America has an *absolute* advantage in producing just about everything, but each country has a range of goods in which it has a *comparative* advantage.

Both sides may complain about the resulting pattern of trade. Mexicans will lament that they are able to compete only on the basis of low wages; Americans will worry that their standard of living will be dragged down by the necessity of competing with cheap Mexican labor. In fact, however, in our example, trade raises real incomes in both countries. Each country imports only those goods in which the other country's relative productivity is higher than its relative wage, implying that the imports cost less in terms of the importing country's labor than what would be required to produce them at home. That is, each country is better off specializing in producing a limited range of goods and importing the rest than it would be if it cut itself off from trade—and this is true regardless of the relative wage rates in the two countries.

Stick with this example for a moment longer, and ask: which country is more competitive? The answer is that it is hard to see what the question means. America has a competitive advantage in some industries, Mexico in others; but neither country has anything that usefully can be considered a problem of overall inability to compete. In fact most economists— including those responsible for the "new trade theory" that underlies Tyson's book—regard "competitiveness" as a non-sense term when applied to countries as a whole.

Does traditional trade theory maintain, then, that everyone gains from free trade? No: it maintains that every *country* gains but allows for the possibility that trade may have strong effects on the distribution of income *within* countries. Loosen up our example, and allow for two kinds of labor, skilled and unskilled, with the relative supply of skilled labor higher in America. Is it possible then that trade, while raising real income for America as a whole, will actually hurt unskilled workers? Indeed it is: one of the classic papers of traditional trade theory was the demonstration by Paul Samuelson and Wolfgang Stolper, more than 50 years ago, that reducing tariffs on labor-intensive goods will reduce real wages unless the domestic losers are compensated by the domestic winners.

Concerns over internal income distribution are, however, a very different thing from supposed issues of national competitiveness. And traditionally economists have had a cynical view of claims that free trade hurts the national interest, seeing such claims as little more than attempts to disguise special interest pleading by wrapping it in the flag.

II

For the last 15 years, a sophisticated critique of this traditional view of international trade has been steadily gaining ground among economists. The "new trade theory" does not discard the insights of traditional trade theory, but it does suggest some qualifications to the case for free trade; it is these qualifications that provide the intellectual basis for *Who's Bashing Whom?*

The new trade theory claims that much of international trade is the result, not of inherent national advantages, but of "increasing returns:" the advantages of large-scale production either at the level of an individual firm or at the level of a national industry. For example, even if all industrial countries were equally talented at producing commercial aircraft, you wouldn't expect them all to get into the business: the economies of scale, both in R&D and in production, are too large to allow more than one or two profitable producers. New trade theorists concede that, at a broad level, trade reflects national resources and character—Canada will never be a coffee exporter—but argue that, at a more detailed level, much trade reflects the way that history and accident get locked in by self-reinforcing advantages. The logic of increasing returns mandates that world production of large commercial aircraft be concentrated *somewhere*; Seattle just happens to be where the roulette wheel came to a stop.

This sounds pretty simple. Why did it require a new theory? Because just talking plausibly about economics is not the same as having a real understanding; for that you need crisp, tightly argued models. And markets subject to increasing returns are, inevitably, much harder to model than diminishing-returns markets like those for wheat or coal. You can't do new trade theory without introducing a heavy element of industrial organization, the often intricate theory that tries to explain the strategic interactions of large firms. It wasn't until about 1980 that theorists were able to offer a convincing blend of industrial organization with international trade.

Once that blend was available, however, it received quick acceptance. New trade theory is now part of the mainstream of economic analysis, to the point where the American Economic

Association's classification system for journal articles now contains a category entitled "Models of trade with increasing returns and imperfect competition," at the same level as "Conventional trade models"—in effect, the new trade theory has become part of the orthodoxy.

What has been accepted, however, is the descriptive part of new trade theory, the story that it tells about the pattern of trade. Its policy implications are much more controversial—and that's where Laura Tyson comes in.

It's obvious that the new trade theory story introduces the possibility that government action can, in effect, *create* comparative advantage. U.S. military procurement in the 50s and 60s did much to create our national advantage in aircraft production, an advantage that is now self-perpetuating (or would be except for the subsidized challenge from Europe's Airbus). In principle, clever government intervention can not only shift the pattern of comparative advantage, but also do so in a way that raises the intervening country's real income at the expense of other countries. The theoretical argument for such predatory policies was first made by the Canadian economists James Brander and Barbara Spencer in the early 1980s and quickly became notorious under the name of "strategic trade policy."

The rhetoric, if not the full intellectual depth, of strategic trade policy has become very popular among politicians and policy entrepreneurs interested in trade. In general, however, we can say that most economists working on international trade have agreed that strategic trade policy can work in principle but have been highly skeptical about its importance and usefulness in practice. I once offered a typology of attitudes on the subject that classified most economists, including new trade theorists, as "cautious non-activists"—willing to do research on strategic trade policy, but not to propose actually doing it, at least right now. Tyson, however, referring to my typology, classifies herself as a "cautious activist," willing to advocate limited moves both to make a US strategic trade policy and to counter the perceived strategic policies of other countries.

What's with all this caution? A large part of the answer is the sheer difficulty of formulating a useful strategic trade policy, or even of evaluating the results of past policies. This difficulty is the main reason why *Who's Bashing Whom?* is such a dense read.

The point is that while all perfect markets are alike, each imperfect market is imperfect in its own way. You can't propose a one-size-fits-all policy for industries as different as aircraft, semiconductors, and telecommunications. Instead, you have to base interventionist proposals on detailed predictions about how firms will change their strategies in response to hypothetical policy changes, how these strategic moves will affect profits, wages, R&D, and so on, and finally, how all of these changes will spill over to the economy at large. To have any hope of doing all this you need lots of detail about the technology, history, and policy environment of an industry— and even then you may, if you admit it to yourself, be at a loss when it comes to making quantitative judgments.

From these difficulties follow two features of *Who's Bashing Whom?*: the density of detail and the surprisingly equivocal tone of its conclusions in each case. Tyson is remarkably guarded about claiming successes for strategic trade policy. In the case study of aircraft, for example, which is arguably the book's centerpiece, we find such hedged statements as this: "In the absence of a more formal modeling effort, it is impossible to conclude that the overall welfare effects of such subsidies have been positive. But there should be no presumption that they have been negative either" (p. 195). In another case study, she has this to say about the Semiconductor Trade Agreement between the U.S. and Japan: "The conventional wisdom is that the SCTA was an unmitigated failure. But the evidence presented here suggests that a more nuanced conclusion is closer to the mark" (p. 132).

I sympathize with her caution. Anyone who has tried the actual business of quantifying the effects of policy in an industry like aircraft knows how quickly your sense that you really understand the industry fades when you start to ask the hard questions. But there is a point that does emerge from virtually all studies that try to quantify the potential gains from strategic trade policy, and I wish that she had made it: while strategic trade policy may work in some cases, from the point of view of the economy as a whole, the stakes are almost certainly quite small.

Let me offer an illustrative calculation. The studies that Tyson cites in support of the proposition that Airbus has been a successful proposition from Europe's point of view depend crucially on the fact that aircraft workers are paid more than seemingly equivalent workers in other industries—without the imputed wage gains, Airbus has cost its sponsors more than it is worth. It is a fact that production workers in high-technology industries are paid about $4000 more per year than those in other industries. If you believe that this is a true premium, and not a reward for hidden quality differences among workers, then every worker shifted into high-technology employment adds $4000 to the gross national product.

Now there are about 3 million workers in U.S. high-technology industries. Imagine that a hugely aggressive strategic trade policy—well beyond anything Tyson proposes—managed to shift an additional million workers out of other employment into the sector. This would then raise national income by $4 billion annually. That sounds like a lot—but it's only $\frac{1}{15}$ of one percent of our $6 trillion GNP. Any real strategic trade policy would surely be both smaller and less successful than this.

You can make other arguments, of course, notably about the indirect payoffs from higher R&D, but it remains difficult to make any plausible argument that the best conceivable strategic trade policy would add more than 1 or 2 billion dollars a year to national income. This puts strategic trade policy as an issue in the same league as pricing policies for ranchers and miners operating on federal land.

Now the fact that a policy issue is not of life-and-death importance does not mean that it should be ignored. As Everett Dirksen said, a billion here, a billion there, and soon you're talking about real money. So by all means let us support the development of promising technologies and bargain toughly with foreign nations we believe are pursuing their own strategic policies. But let us maintain the right perspective and not imagine ourselves in the midst of some apocalyptic struggle over global supremacy.

Unfortunately, many people do believe that we are in the midst of such a struggle. The big risk with a book like *Who's Bashing Whom?* is that it will play into their misconceptions.

III

Ross Perot set some kind of new standard for discussion of trade policy when, during the Presidential debates, he spoke of the "giant sucking sound" of jobs moving south after free trade with Mexico. The worrisome thing about the discussion of U.S. trade policy today is, however, that many people who believe themselves to be sophisticated and forward-looking hold views about the U.S. role in the world economy that are almost as crude as Perot's.

Over the past decade or so, a deeply misconceived ideology of international trade has taken hold of much of the public discussion of economic issues in general. This ideology doesn't have a generally accepted name, so let me give it one: "competitive internationalism," or CI, for short.

The quintessential CI statement came from none other than President Clinton himself, who told a Silicon Valley audience, "Now the United States is like a big corporation in the world economy." That is, CI theorists see our economic problem as crucially one of competing with foreign rivals and blame our economic difficulties on a lack of international competitiveness—precisely what both traditional and new trade theorists say is nonsense.

In this context, it is important to notice what Tyson's book does *not* say. It does not say that the US has suffered a major erosion of its industrial base due to international competition; that the loss of good industrial jobs is largely responsible for the stagnation of U.S. living standards; that competition from low-wage workers abroad is responsible for declining real wages of many U.S. workers; or that the U.S. needs to regain its productivity edge if it is going be competitive in the global economy.

These omissions are important, because many influential people believe in these propositions, and they probably imagine that Laura Tyson shares their beliefs. No support for any of these ideas, however, may be found in *Who's Bashing Whom?* for a very good reason. As a conscientious economist, Tyson knows that they are all flatly untrue.

Take, for example, the question of deindustrialization. There is no question that manufacturing plays a smaller role in the U.S. economy than it used to, accounting for only 17 percent of jobs in 1991 versus 27 percent in 1968. During the economic summit in December 1992, President-elect Bill Clinton, no doubt influenced by the CI theorists close to him (or perhaps we should simply regard the president himself as a competitive internationalist), mused repeatedly on his desire to see U.S.

manufacturing become more competitive and regain the lost jobs. But the truth is that international competition has almost nothing to do with that downward trend: even if the US were to eliminate its trade deficit in manufactures and return to the roughly balanced trade of a generation ago, the manufacturing share of employment would rise only to about 17.5 percent.

The political and media influence of CI poses a dilemma for economists who want to have a benign influence on policy, especially if they happen to be liberals. Should they vent their feelings of intellectual outrage over seeing crude fallacies treated as sophisticated insight? In 1983, when the industrial policy ideas of competitive internationalists like Robert Reich and Lester Thurow were highly fashionable among what were then known as "Atari Democrats," a brilliant young liberal economist named Lawrence Summers could not restrain his scorn, referring to their ideas as "economic laetrile" and "chiropractic economics." He was honest then; but his ridicule did little to slow the spread of the ideas he thought so foolish, and Summers, widely expected to become Bill Clinton's chief economic adviser, didn't get the job.

Laura Tyson has followed a very different approach. Since the early 1980s she has taken on the role of ambassador between the new trade theory and competitive internationalism. In a long series of books and articles, of which *Who's Bashing Whom?* is the culmination, she has in effect shuttled between the two worlds. Her long-standing connection with the Berkeley Roundtable on International Economics, a relatively mild-mannered CI think tank, has given her a forum in which to try to convince at least some of that school to base their interventionist case on sophisticated ideas rather than a know-nothing rejection of all economics. At the same time, she has maintained her standing as a mainstream economist and used that standing to try to convince her colleagues to listen to and educate competitive internationalists rather than disdain them.

In fact, *Who's Bashing Whom?* may be regarded as a diplomatic as well as a scholarly document. It is a solid piece of mainstream modern international economics. Its interventionist slant is well within the bounds of polite conversation among the professorial class. But its tone and style are designed to appeal to competitive internationalists. One surmises that Tyson hoped that her book would help bring the two factions together.

I wish her luck, but I doubt that she'll succeed. *Who's Bashing Whom?* is not her first effort along these lines; indeed, she has been engaged in intellectual shuttle diplomacy for at least ten years. Judging from what the leading competitive internationalists have written, however, she has made no progress at all in convincing them to pay attention to the new trade theory she so much admires. Robert Reich had a best-seller, *The Work of Nations,* in 1991; Thurow had a blockbuster, *Head to Head,* in 1992; neither book mentions increasing returns—or for that matter, comparative advantage.

So one worries about the ultimate effect of *Who's Bashing Whom?* Will it help move the US to a sophisticated trade strategy? Or will it end up providing an intellectual gloss for a crudely belligerent policy—a policy formulated by people who have not transcended conventional wisdom on international trade, but rather literally don't know the first thing about it?

8   What Do Undergrads
         Need to Know about
         Trade?

Few of the undergraduates who take an introductory course in
economics will go on to graduate study in the field, and indeed
most will not even take any higher-level economics courses. So
what they learn about economics will be what they get in that
first course. It is now more important than ever before that
their basic training include a solid grounding in the principles
of international trade.

I could justify this assertion by pointing out that international trade is now more important to the U.S. economy than it
used to be. But there is another reason, which I think is even
more important: the increased *perception* among the general
public that international trade is a vital subject. We live in a
time in which Americans are obsessed with international competition, in which Lester Thurow's *Head to Head* is the non-
fiction best-seller, and Michael Crichton's *Rising Sun* tops the
fiction list. The news media and the business literature are
saturated with discussions of America's role in the world
economy.

The problem is that most of what a student is likely to read
or hear about international economics is nonsense. What I want

Reprinted by permission from *American Economic Review* (May 1993): 23–26.

to argue in this paper is that the most important thing to teach our undergrads about trade is how to detect that nonsense. That is, our primary mission should be to vaccinate the minds of our undergraduates against the misconceptions that are so predominant in what passes for educated discussion about international trade.

I   The Rhetoric of Pop Internationalism

As a starting point, I would like to quote a typical statement about international economics. (Please ignore the numbers for a moment.) Here it is: "We need a new economic paradigm, because today America is part of a truly global economy.[1] To maintain its standard of living, America now has to learn to compete in an ever tougher world marketplace.[2] That's why high productivity and product quality have become essential.[3] We need to move the American economy into the high-value sectors[4] that will generate jobs[5] for the future. And the only way we can be competitive in the new global economy is if we forge a new partnership between government and business."[6]

OK, I confess: it's not a real quotation. I made it up as a sort of compendium of popular misconceptions about international trade. But it certainly sounds like the sort of thing one reads or hears all the time—it is very close in content and style to the still-influential manifesto by Ira Magaziner and Robert Reich (1982), or for that matter to the presentation made by Apple Computer's John Sculley at President-elect Clinton's Economic Conference last December. People who say things like this believe themselves to be smart, sophisticated, and forward-looking. They do not know that they are repeating a set of misleading clichés that I will dub "pop internationalism."

It is fairly easy to understand why pop internationalism has so much popular appeal. In effect, it portrays America as being like a corporation that used to have a lot of monopoly power, and could therefore earn comfortable profits in spite of sloppy business practices, but is now facing an onslaught from new competitors. A lot of companies are in that position these days (though the new competitors are not necessarily foreign), and so the image rings true.

Unfortunately, it's a grossly misleading image, because a national economy bears very little resemblance to a corporation. And the ground-level view of businessmen is deeply uninformative about the inherently general-equilibrium issues of international economics.

So what do undergrads need to know about trade? They need to know that pop internationalism is nonsense—and they need to know *why* it is nonsense.

II   Common Misconceptions

I inserted numbers into my imaginary quotation to mark six currently popular misconceptions that can and should be dispelled in an introductory economics course.

1. "We need a new paradigm...." Pop internationalism proclaims that everything is different now that the United States is an open economy. Probably the most important single insight that an introductory course can convey about international economics is that it does *not* change the basics: trade is just another economic activity, subject to the same principles as anything else.

James Ingram's (1983) textbook on international trade contains a lovely parable. He imagines that an entrepreneur starts a new business that uses a secret technology to convert U.S. wheat, lumber, and so on into cheap high-quality consumer goods. The entrepreneur is hailed as an industrial hero; although some of his domestic competitors are hurt, everyone accepts that occasional dislocations are the price of a free-market economy. But then an investigative reporter discovers that what he is really doing is shipping the wheat and lumber to Asia and using the proceeds to buy manufactured goods—whereupon he is denounced as a fraud who is destroying American jobs. The point, of course, is that international trade is an economic activity like any other and can indeed usefully be thought of as a kind of production process that transforms exports into imports.

It might, incidentally, also be a good thing if undergrads got a more realistic quantitative sense than the pop internationalists seem to have of the limited extent to which the United States actually has become a part of a global economy. The fact is that imports and exports are still only about one-eighth of output, and at least two-thirds of our value-added consists of nontradable goods and services. Moreover, one should have some historical perspective with which to counter the silly claims that our current situation is completely unprecedented: the United States is not now and may never be as open to trade as the United Kingdom has been since the reign of Queen Victoria.

2. "Competing in the world marketplace:" One of the most popular, enduring misconceptions of practical men is that countries are in competition with each other in the same way that companies in the same business are in competition. Ricardo already knew better in 1817. An introductory economics course should drive home to students the point that international trade is not about competition, it is about mutually beneficial exchange. Even more fundamentally, we should be able to teach students that imports, not exports, are the purpose of trade. That is, what a country gains from trade is the ability to import things it wants. Exports are not an objective in and of themselves: the need to export is a burden that a country must

bear because its import suppliers are crass enough to demand payment.

One of the distressing things about the tyranny of pop internationalism is that there has been a kind of Gresham's Law in which bad concepts drive out good. Lester Thurow is a trained economist, who understands comparative advantage. Yet his recent book has been a best-seller largely because it vigorously propounds concepts that unintentionally (one hopes) pander to the clichés of pop internationalism: "Niche competition is win—win. Everyone has a place where he or she can excel; no one is going to be driven out of business. Head-to-head competition is win—lose." (Thurow, 1992 p. 30). We should try to instill in undergrads a visceral negative reaction to statements like this.

3. "Productivity:" Students should learn that high productivity is beneficial, not because it helps a country to compete with other countries, but because it lets a country produce and therefore consume more. This would be true in a closed economy; it is no more and no less true in an open economy; but that is not what pop internationalists believe.

I have found it useful to offer students the following thought experiment. First, imagine a world in which productivity rises by 1 percent annually in all countries. What will be the trend in the U.S. standard of living? Students have no trouble agreeing that it will rise by 1 percent per year. Now, however, suppose that while the United States continues to raise its productivity by only 1 percent per year, the rest of the world manages to achieve 3-percent productivity growth. What is the trend in our living standard?

The correct answer is that the trend is still 1 percent, except possibly for some subtle effects via our terms of trade: and as an empirical matter changes in the U.S. terms of trade have had virtually no impact on the trend in our living standards over the past few decades. But very few students reach that conclusion—which is not surprising, since virtually everything they read or hear outside of class conveys the image of international trade as a competitive sport.

An anecdote: when I published an op-ed piece in the *New York Times* last year, I emphasized the importance of rising productivity. The editorial assistant I dealt with insisted that I should "explain" that we need to be productive "to compete in the global economy." He was reluctant to publish the piece unless I added the phrase—he said it was necessary so that readers could understand why productivity is important. We need to try to turn out a generation of students who not only don't need that kind of explanation, but understand why it's wrong.

4. "High-value sectors:" Pop internationalists believe that international competition is a struggle over who gets the "high-value" sectors. "Our country's real income can rise only if (1) its labor and capital increasingly flow toward businesses that add greater value per employee and (2) we maintain a position in these businesses that is superior to that of our international competitors" (Magaziner and Reich. 1982 p. 4).

I think it should be possible to teach students why this is a silly concept. Take, for example, a simple two-good Ricardian model in which one country is more productive in both industries than the other. (I have in mind the one used in Krugman and Maurice Obstfeld [1991 pp. 20–1]. The more productive country will, of course, have a higher wage rate, and therefore whatever sector that country specializes in will be "high value," that is, will have higher value-added per worker. Does this mean that the country's high living standard is the result of being in the right sector, or that the poorer country would be richer if it tried to emulate the other's pattern of specialization? Of course not.

5. "Jobs:" One thing that both friends and foes of free trade seem to agree on is that the central issue is employment. George Bush declared the objective of his ill-starred trip to Japan to be "jobs, jobs, jobs;" both sides in the debate over the North American Free Trade Agreement try to make their case in terms of job creation. And an astonishing number of free-traders think that the reason protectionism is bad is that it causes depressions.

It should be possible to emphasize to students that the level of employment is a macroeconomic issue, depending in the short run on aggregate demand and depending in the long run on the natural rate of unemployment, with microeconomic policies like tariffs having little net effect. Trade policy should be debated in terms of its impact on efficiency, not in terms of phony numbers about jobs created or lost.

6. "A new partnership:" The bottom line for many pop internationalists is that since U.S. firms are competing with foreigners instead of each other, the U.S. government should turn from its alleged adversarial position to one of supporting our firms against their foreign rivals. A more sophisticated pop internationalist like Robert Reich (1991) realizes that the interests of U.S. *firms* are not the same as those of U.S. *workers* (you may find it hard to believe that anyone needed to point this out, but among pop internationalists this was viewed as a deep and controversial insight), but still accepts the basic premise that the U.S. government should help our industries compete.

What we should be able to teach our students is that the main competition going on is one of U.S. industries against *each other*, over which sector is going to get the scarce resources of capital, skill, and, yes, labor. Government support of an industry may help that industry compete against foreigners, but it also draws resources away from other domestic industries. That is, the increased importance of international trade does not change the fact the government cannot favor one domestic industry except at the expense of others.

Now there are reasons, such as external economies, why a preference for some industries over others may be justified. But this would be true in a closed economy, too. Students need to understand that the growth of world trade provides no additional support for the proposition that our government should become an active friend to domestic industry.

III What We Should Teach

By now the thrust of my discussion should be clear. For the bulk of our economics students, our objective should be to equip them to respond intelligently to popular discussion of economic issues. A lot of that discussion will be about international trade, so international trade should be an important part of the curriculum.

What is crucial, however, is to understand that the level of public discussion is extremely primitive. Indeed, it has sunk so low that people who repeat silly clichés often imagine themselves to be sophisticated. That means that our courses need to drive home as clearly as possible the basics. Offer curves and Rybczinski effects are lovely things. What most students need to be prepared for, however, is a world in which TV "experts," best-selling authors, and $30,000-a-day consultants do not understand budget constraints, let alone comparative advantage.

The last 15 years have been a golden age of innovation in international economics. I must somewhat depressingly conclude, however, that this innovative stuff is not a priority for today's undergraduates. In the last decade of the 20th century, the essential things to teach students are still the insights of

Hume and Ricardo. That is, we need to teach them that trade deficits are self-correcting and that the benefits of trade do not depend on a country having an absolute advantage over its rivals. If we can teach undergrads to wince when they hear someone talk about "competitiveness," we will have done our nation a great service.

References

Crichton, Michael, *Rising Sun*, New York: Knopf, 1992.

Ingram, James, *International Economics*, New York: Wiley, 1983.

Krugman, Paul and Obstfeld, Maurice, *International Economics: Theory and Policy*, New York: Harper Collins. 1991.

Magaziner, Ira and Reich, Robert, *Minding America's Business*, New York: Random House, 1982.

Reich, Robert, *The Work of Nations*, New York: Knopf, 1991.

Thurow, Lester, *Head to Head*, New York: William Morrow, 1992.

III

The Emerging World

9   Challenging
       Conventional
       Wisdom

Good morning. Before I begin my talk, let me express my appreciation to the organizers and sponsors of this conference for giving me the opportunity to speak to you. Let me also act a little bit like a Japanese and begin with an apology. I have been asked to speak about the economic outlook, with reference not only to the world at large but also to Mexico in particular. I will do my best to cover that very large area in the next hour or so. But I would be the first to admit that I am not an expert on the Mexican economy. I will therefore try to talk about Mexico in *context*, to show how Mexican experience fits into the broader patterns we see in the world as a whole. If this means that I seem to say too little about the specifics of Mexican developments, I apologize; and I am sure that we will be able to remedy some of that vagueness during the question-and-answer period later this morning.

With that disclaimer, then, let us turn to the economic outlook, for the world in general. North America, more specifically, and Mexico, in particular. Or rather, let us get ready to look at that economic outlook: for there is some preliminary business we need to resolve first.

The author presented this speech in Mexico City, March 1993.

On Questioning Conventional Wisdom

I expect that many people here have heard of the late economist Carlos Diaz-Alejandro. Professor Diaz was not only a fine
economist, he was something very unusual in that profession, a
man of wisdom. And he pointed out something that is very
important if you want to try to make good judgments about
the world economy: the difference between real economic
knowledge and the conventional wisdom that prevails at any
given time.

What Diaz realized was that most of the time there is a set
of ideas that most serious people who worry about international economic policy believe—a set of ideas that goes far
beyond what economic research really tells us. Indeed, sometimes what all serious people believe is flatly in contradiction
of what the best research says. For example, top officials in the
advanced countries and the most influential journalists agree
that international policy coordination through the G7 is extremely important if we are to get out of the current global
slowdown. They believe this in spite of the fact that nobody
who has tried to produce a quantitative assessment of the
benefits of macroeconomic policy coordination has been able
to come up with any evidence that such coordination produces
significant gains.

If it isn't based on the best evidence, then, where does
conventional wisdom about economic policy come from? It is
partly driven by economic analysis—I don't mean to say that
research is completely ignored—and partly driven by recent
economic experience. To a large extent, however, it is the
result of the fact that serious people talk mostly to each other
and tend to believe what they hear. Suppose, to take an
example that is obviously not chosen at random, that it
becomes standard for speakers at meetings where influential

people gather—at G7 ministerials, or Trilateral Commission plenaries, at Davos or at Jackson Hole—to say the following: "Devaluation is not an effective economic strategy; any temporary gains in competitiveness are quickly dissipated in inflation, and it leaves the real problems unsolved." People who say something like this may be drawing, to some extent, on what they know about the failures of recent devaluations, but their confidence in what they say comes not so much from solid evidence as from the fact that so many other important people are saying the same thing. You get my point: conventional wisdom, while to some extent based on real evidence, has a strong element of sheer fashion to it.

Now the conventional wisdom that currently dominates thinking about international economic affairs has a name: John Williamson, of the Institute for International Economics, has called it the "Washington view." (That's not because it comes from the U.S. government; it is more because it comes from Washington-based international institutions like the IMF, the World Bank, the Inter-American Development Bank, and so on. And important people in international economic affairs tend to meet in Washington more often than anywhere else.)

I'll describe the Washington view in a minute. The point I would like you to bear in mind, however, is that it is not the first such conventional wisdom to dominate international economic discussion, nor the second, nor the third. In fact, I would count at least four "conventional wisdoms" on economic policy since the early 20th century.

The first conventional wisdom was that of the era of laissez-faire. If you go back to the 1920s, you find that responsible people both in industrial countries and in what we would now call developing countries believed in a very simple doctrine: free markets and sound money. If you got these things right, they believed, the economy would take care of itself.

By the 1940s, the conventional wisdom had almost completely reversed. The perceived successes of the Soviet Union
and the obvious failures of capitalism in the 1930s, together
with a new interventionism in economic theory more generally, led to the solidification of a new conventional wisdom.
The new doctrine—accepted by international organizations
like the World Bank as well as policymakers in developing
countries—called for an active economic development strategy plus *controlled* money. That is, the responsible thing for
a country was now to plan its economic growth, which in
developing countries usually meant industrializing via import-
substitution policies; since such policies often seemed to run
into balance of payments problems, the import substitution
should be backed by foreign exchange controls.

By the 1970s, there was widespread disillusionment with
government action in general and import substitution in particular. So the next conventional wisdom took shape. It called for
free-market *microeconomic* policies—doing away with import
substitution—together with Keynesian *macroeconomic* policies.
For advanced countries, this meant deregulation and competitive markets but active monetary and fiscal policies to stabilize
the economy. The typical '70s prescription for a developing
country was "liberalization plus devaluation": liberalization to
do away with what were now widely seen as the horrors of
import substitution, devaluation to allow liberalization to proceed without balance of payments crisis or recession.

By the late 1980s, however, experiences in both advanced
countries and developing countries led to disillusionment with
the active side of this policy pairing. Free markets looked better
than ever, with the success of export-oriented industrialization
in some developing countries and the spectacular breakup of
Communism. But active monetary, fiscal, and exchange rate
policies were widely seen as discredited by the experience of

inflation. And so by the late 1980s a new conventional wisdom had taken hold, calling for—guess what!—free markets and sound money.

Around 1990 this new/old conventional wisdom had taken almost complete hold of discussion among serious people. (By serious people I mean people who either are finance ministers or actually enjoy talking to them.) But like any conventional wisdom, it was based more on the circular process of important people reinforcing each other's current dogma than on really solid evidence.

And now I'm ready to talk about the current economic outlook, because it seems to me that you can't make sense of the current state of the world—or of Mexico—without realizing that the last few years have deeply challenged the conventional wisdom that was almost unquestioned in 1990.

What People Thought They Knew

Let's turn the clock back to 1990 for a moment. What did the world look like, at least to those who believed in the conventional wisdom?

In the first place, what serious people saw almost everywhere was the triumph of free-market ideas. The fall of Communism obviously dominated the headlines. For those who were looking at more mundane policy issues, however, the successes of free-market, sound-money policies in market economies were what supported the conventional wisdom.

Let's start with what was seen as the evidence in favor of free markets.

It's hard to remember this now, but only three years ago there was widespread acceptance of the view that both Ronald Reagan and Margaret Thatcher had been quite successful in their respective countries. In both countries the recessions of the early 1980s had given way to sustained recoveries. In the United States that recovery had brought unemployment to its lowest level in more than 15 years, without any surge in inflation; and while overall productivity growth was still disappointing, there had been a noticeable revival in both the productivity and the international competitiveness of manufacturing. In the United Kingdom the mid-1980s had been marked by a revival of productivity growth, and the late 1980s had finally seen some reduction in the high unemployment of the Thatcher years.

In other words, while many serious people didn't like Reagan or Thatcher, while many people were upset about the social consequences of their policies, the general view was that their free-market policies had worked pretty well.

We should also mention the effects of "1992" in Europe— or more to the point, the effects of the announcement of plans to remove remaining barriers to trade within Europe. The plan to establish a unified market was announced in 1987 and was almost immediately followed by a surge in investment that brought European unemployment rates down for the first time since the early 1970s. What better demonstration could one have of the virtues of free trade?

If the results of free-market policies in advanced countries seemed pretty good, the results in developing countries seemed even better. By 1990 the East Asian success story had finally really penetrated the consciousness of the educated public. Unplanned, even chaotic industrialization aimed at export markets, often overseen not by the local government but by the same foreign multinationals that had been cast as villains only a few years before, was now obviously leading to rapid growth in many countries—nor was it just tiny, cohesive nations like Singapore or even medium-sized ones like Korea or Taiwan. Free-market development was transforming the economic prospects of big countries, like Indonesia and huge ones, like China.

So in 1990 the free market looked pretty good, North and South. What about sound money?

Here the overwhelmingly important experience was the apparent success of the European Monetary System. When the EMS was founded in 1979, most observers gave it little chance of succeeding. From about 1982 on, however, the EMS became a remarkably stable set of exchange rates. European countries that devalued, like France or Sweden, soon found themselves with inflation problems; in order to restore credibility, they committed themselves to fixed rates without realignment thereafter. By 1987, all of Europe, except the United Kingdom, was apparently functioning quite well with rates as fixed as they ever were under the Bretton Woods system. By 1990, it was common for sensible people to say firmly that devaluation was no longer a useful policy option. And Europe seemed on an inevitable path to full monetary union.

Again, these apparent lessons for the advanced countries were reinforced by different but seemingly related experiences in the developing world. The debt crisis in the developing world led to the emergence of very high inflation rates; we used to regard the study of hyperinflation as a historical exercise that involved looking at data from the 1920s, but in the 1980s it became a matter of current events. In the efforts to control high inflation, exchange rate targets came to play an important role. And those countries that attempted to devalue their way out of the debt-induced slump, like Brazil, were clearly seen to pay a price in high inflation.

You'll notice that I am being very selective in this list of evidence. If you wanted to, you could quite easily have presented some things that happened in the 1980s as reasons not to believe in the conventional wisdom. For example, the results of the depreciation of the U.S. dollar from 1985 to 1987 did not at all fit the new story about why devaluation doesn't work. The dollar declined by about 30 percent on average, by more than 50 percent against the mark and the yen; that decline did not produce a surge in inflation, but it did produce a surge in exports.

The point, however, is that conventional wisdom is always much stronger than the real evidence. As little as two years ago, a lot of important people had no doubts about the equation *Free Markets* + *Sound Money* = *Prosperity*.

Unfortunately, life isn't that simple; and that's what we've found out in the last couple of years.

The Erosion of Conventional Wisdom in Advanced Countries

The new disillusionment with what was until a little while ago the dominant conventional wisdom has so far been confined to advanced country affairs. That isn't going to last. In fact, the conclusion of my talk, the part that is going to get some people upset, will be about what the dissolution of the conventional wisdom means for developing countries. But let me stay with the rich nations for now.

Let's start with the United States. Obviously Bill Clinton, a liberal who does not believe in free markets as the solution to all problems, won the last election. There's much more to what has happened in the United States than simply an election result, however. What has happened is a full rejection, by a heavy majority of the public, of the whole ideology that dominated U.S. politics during the last 12 years. Let me offer two pieces of evidence for just how fundamental the change is. First, have you noticed that Ronald Reagan has disappeared? It's not just that he is personally rarely seen. The important thing is that nobody mentions him. Only a few years ago he was one of the most popular presidents in U.S. history, acclaimed as a conservative hero. Today, I think it is fair to say that most Americans, which, by definition, includes a lot of people who voted for him, are embarrassed by the memory of the Reagan era and would just as soon forget that it happened.

Second, if you follow U.S. politics at all, you will have noticed that the conservatives seem at a complete loss for ideas. The new president is doing things that everyone thought were political suicide—raising taxes not only on the rich but on the middle class, cutting benefits, and breaking his campaign promises by doing so—and yet the right in the United States seems to be *unable to mobilize* against him. It turns out that the free-market ideology that seemed so strong was like a dead tree that is still standing: once knocked over by a strong wind, it turns out to be hollow inside.

What happened in the U.S. was that the recession and unemployment of 1990–1992 focussed the attention of voters, not just on their immediate problems, but on the failure of the previous twelve years to produce any real rise in their standard of living. That is, they became aware that the much-trumpeted success of free-market policies was more a matter of rhetoric than of reality. And so they turned their backs on conservatives.

Of course I have just told you what President Clinton is against, but not what he's for; but let me hold off on that for a little while. The important point for now is that the U.S. government is currently headed by people who do not, by and large, accept the conventional wisdom of the "Washington view."

Events have been different in Europe, but there too the conventional wisdom has fallen victim to events. In Europe, of course, the decisive events have been those associated with the breakup of the European Monetary System and the apparent failure of the Maastricht Treaty.

I think that it is now fair to say that the belief among Europeans—that they had matured past the point where exchange rate devaluations were necessary or even useful—was based on a misunderstanding. They looked at the success of the European Monetary System between 1982 and 1990 and saw it as a fundamental endorsement of sound money, rather than realizing that it was a temporary success based on special circumstances.

In retrospect, we can say that fixed exchange rates worked in Europe for a while because they were convenient. For most of the 1980s, inflation was the problem paramount in European minds. France, Italy, and, eventually, the United Kingdom needed an anchor to fight their historical tendency toward inflation, and found that anchor by pegging their currencies to the German mark. This visible commitment gained them immediate credibility with the financial markets, reflected in lower interest rates, and may have helped reduce inflation rates at a bit less cost in unemployment than would have been possible without the EMS.

The problem with the European system was that it forced all countries to have the same monetary policy, and placed control of that policy in German hands. During the 1980s, this wasn't a problem, because all of the countries shared the same goals. Sooner or later, however, a crisis was bound to come.

Most people probably already know what the nature of the crisis was. When Germany reunified, the massive costs of supporting and rebuilding the East meant a huge fiscal expansion. To prevent that expansion from causing inflation, Germany adopted very tight money policies. The problem was that other European countries were forced to match the tight money without the fiscal expansion, which meant a severe recession that spread across all of the continent, eventually touching Germany itself.

The obvious answer to this problem was a revaluation of the mark, or, equivalently, a devaluation of the other currencies in Europe. But this wasn't allowed by the conventional wisdom, which said that devaluations don't work and are simply inflationary. And no serious person wants to be seen challenging the conventional wisdom! As late as September 14 of last year, Britain's Chancellor of the Exchequer, Norman Lamont, was insisting publicly that Britain was not considering a devaluation of the pound under any circumstances. Two days later, of course, the pound was taken out of the exchange rate mechanism. (A few days later the Chancellor was insisting that he had never really wanted to defend the pound, and that he was "singing in the bath" the day after it fell. This was an unfortunate omen for the credibility of policymakers everywhere.)

I'd like to tell one personal story to illustrate the extent to which people who want to seem serious are unwilling to question the conventional wisdom. A few weeks after the fall of the British pound, I visited Sweden on a lecture tour. It seemed obvious to me that the Swedish situation bore a strong basic resemblance to the British one: a severe recession brought on by the need to match German interest rates, with the Swedish currency clearly overvalued by normal standards—especially given the recent devaluations by the United Kingdom and Finland. Indeed, there was a speculative attack on the Swedish crown just after the U.K. crisis, which was beaten back only by pusing short-term interest rates up to 500 percent. But nobody in the Swedish establishment, *including economic experts outside the government*, was willing even to discuss the possibility that currency devaluation should be part of a recovery strategy. As a result, I found myself rather unexpectedly on television and in the newspapers, not because I was saying anything that wasn't obvious, but because here was a real, live economist with good credentials actually willing to say something different. The government's officials were, of course, dismissive; they informed me that I didn't understand the situation. And it was almost two months before another speculative attack actually forced them to allow the currency to depreciate.

Of course I don't see any parallel with what happened to me in Sweden and my situation here—no parallel at all.

Anyway, I think that I have made my point. A few years ago the conventional wisdom of free markets and sound money was treated by many people as revealed truth, even though there was actually a lot of contrary evidence. And policymakers are extremely reluctant to change their collective minds or admit that they themselves had been wrong. Nonetheless, in both the United States and Europe, the "Washington view" has been badly eroded recently, at least insofar as it applies to advanced countries.

But what about developing countries? That's a somewhat different story.

The Perils of Success in the Developing World

Let me now change focus once again, and look at the experience of developing countries over the past decade.

Obviously, developing countries are not all alike, except in the fact that they have lower per capita income than advanced countries. But we can divide many, if not all, developing countries into three classes in terms of their experience in the last 10 years.

First, there are the unambiguous success stories, mostly Asian nations that have been engaging in rapid growth through export-oriented manufacturing. The giant of this class is China, but a number of other countries have managed to do very well recently.

At the other extreme are the disaster stories—many, though not all, in Africa. These countries started poor and got poorer. Indeed, calling them "developing" is starting to sound like a bad joke.

In between are a number of countries that did very badly during much of the 1980s but are doing much better recently. In this class are Chile, Argentina, and, of course, Mexico.

Why did these countries do so much better in the last few years? The short answer is, of course, debt reduction and policy reform; but that's too short an answer, because it fails to reveal the strangeness of the process and some of the weaknesses involved.

Some of what I am about to say may seem to disparage the achievements of reformers in developing countries, in general, and Mexico, in particular. This is not my intention. The reforms undertaken here and elsewhere show astonishing political achievements and good economic policies. The point is not to disparage the reforms but to point out that, in the short run, they worked better than they deserved, and that some of that excessive policy dividend may have to be paid back.

Still, the reforms were impressive. The Chilean story is old history, and one cannot really approve of the political methods used to achieve free-market reforms and an opening of the economy. Still, the impressive thing is that Chile was able to restore democracy without returning to its bad old interventionist ways; and Chile, perhaps uniquely among the non-Asian reforming countries, is showing signs of a takeoff into Asian rates of growth.

In Mexico there was a dramatic trade liberalization between 1985 and 1989. The fraction of imports subject to licenses fell from more than 90 to less than 25 percent, the maximum tariff was cut by 3/4, and even the average tariff fell by half. Add in the wave of privatization, and one has a major economic reform.

Most recently Argentina has joined the reform path, cutting tariffs by more than 60 percent.

Why were such reforms politically possible? It is clear that the conventional wisdom played a crucial role. If trade liberalization is presented as a detailed, microeconomic policy, the industries that stand to lose will be well-informed and vociferous in their opposition, while those who stand to gain will be diffuse and usually ineffective. What reformers in a number of countries were able to do, however, was to present trade liberalization as part of a package that was presumed to yield large gains to the country as a whole. That is, it wasn't presented as "Let's open up imports in these 20 industries and there will be efficiency gains"; that kind of argument doesn't work very well in ordinary times. Instead, it was "We have to follow the strategy that everyone serious knows works: free markets—including free trade—and sound money, leading to rapid economic growth." It is a unified package, and it has been adopted by countries where one would have thought such change was impossible.

The packages have also, by and large, worked—if anything, worked too well.

Let's consider Mexico. The turning point for Mexico was the debt-reduction package negotiated under the Brady Plan. That debt reduction was intelligently handled: Mexico negotiated effectively and toughly with its creditors, and the mechanism of debt reduction was a good one. (In fact, I give Mexico's debt negotiators credit not just for making a good deal for themselves but for saving the whole Brady Plan. The original U.S. plan was confused and unworkable; it was Mexico that devised an intelligent way of reducing debt without giving banks a windfall, providing a blueprint for subsequent debt deals.)

Everyone realized, however, that the actual debt relief under the Mexican debt package was fairly small. It was not nearly enough to make much direct difference to Mexico's growth prospects.

And yet what actually followed the debt reduction was a transformation of the economic picture. With stunning speed, Mexico's problems seemed to melt away. Internal real interest rates were 30–40 percent before the debt deal, with the payments on internal debt a major source of fiscal pressure; they fell to 5–10 percent almost immediately. Mexico had been shut out of international financial markets since 1982; soon after the debt deal, large-scale voluntary capital inflows resumed on an ever-growing scale. And, of course, growth resumed in the long-stagnant economy.

Why did a seemingly modest debt reduction spark such a major change in the economic environment? I think we all know the answer: international investors saw the debt deal as part of a package of reforms that they believed would work. Debt reduction went along with free markets and sound money; free markets and sound money mean prosperity; and so capital flows into the country that follows the right path.

Mexico was not alone in this experience. One of the big surprises of the early 1990s has been the resurgence of private capital flows to selected developing countries. Bank loans to governments and guaranteed firms are, of course, outmoded since the debt crisis; but direct investment, equity investment, and bond purchases are in. The countries that are favored recipients of the new wave of capital are the countries engaged in economic reform in accord with the conventional wisdom. The point is, of course, that players in the financial markets, like the serious people who make policy, believe the conventional wisdom.

What this means is that for the last few years reformers in developing countries have gotten rewarded—not in the long run, when their reforms will begin to bear fruit in a fundamental improvement in their economies, but immediately, as a sort of advance payment from the financial markets. Given this immediate gratification, it is not surprising that there has been much less questioning of the conventional wisdom in developing countries than in the advanced nations of North America and Europe.

And yet there is clearly something unhealthy about reforms that seem to work, not because they have really proved themselves, but because international investors believe in the conventional wisdom on which they are based. What if the conventional wisdom isn't right? Or even if it's basically right, what if the real payoff to free markets and sound money is a longer time coming than financial markets seem to believe? Then there is a risk that things will go seriously wrong. And they will go even worse if the policymakers in the developing countries are too hesitant to admit that at least some parts of the conventional wisdom are wrong.

So the time has now come to talk about the threats that I now see developing in the world economy.

Emerging Threats

A few months ago, there were some reasonable people who feared that the whole world economy might be headed into a persistent slump, with the usual remedies not working. I think, though I'm not totally sure, that this danger is past. The U.S. economy seems to have entered a phase of real recovery. Employment growth has been slow until recently, but job growth has finally picked up. Europe is still sliding, but there are hopeful signs. In particular, Britain's decision to let the pound sink seems to be working on two levels. Britain itself appears to be on the verge of a real recovery; and Germany, facing competition from devalued Britain and Italy, is being forced to cut its own interest rates. From a short-run and even a medium-run point of view, the breakup of fixed exchange rates within Europe is good news for the world economy.

Moreover, there are some signs that long-run trends are turning even more favorable. In the United States, in particular, there has been a surge in productivity. We don't know yet how long the surge will last, but I am impressed by the evidence that something fundamental is happening, such as the applications of modern technology in office work and the service sector. If the productivity takeoff turns out to be sustained, it will mean steadily rising living standards in the United States and in any other countries that share in this revolution. And if prosperous countries are more responsible and generous, this could eventually mean a world economy that works better as a whole.

For the time being, however, things are not so good. And while a severe global economic slump is now unlikely, there is a new risk: an epidemic of protectionism.

Now we have heard a lot of talk about the risks of protectionism in the last few years. Many people see it as an inevitable consequence of the growing conflicts of interest between the major players in the world economy—that was, for example, the central message of Lester Thurow's recent best-selling book, *Head to Head*. I'd like to take a moment out to criticize what many people say about the motives for protectionism before talking about what I think are the real risks.

Many people now say two things about trade conflict. First, they see it as a matter of real conflicts of interest between

America, Europe, and Japan. Second, they visualize a world of three great trading blocs, internally unified but in bitter conflict. The first of these views is entirely wrong; and I don't think that the three-bloc world is at all a good picture of what lies ahead.

In reality, the true conflicts of interest between advanced nations over trade policy are very small. The United States and Europe are deeply divided over farm policy; but the fact is that if Europe gave in to American demands, the main benefits would go to European consumers and taxpayers. A huge fuss has been made over Europe's subsidy to Airbus, but even on the maximum calculation, Europe's subsidies to high technology industries do not reduce U.S. real income by as much as 1/20 of 1 percent. That doesn't mean that there won't be bitter and destructive trade conflicts, but it means that they don't *have* to happen—they will depend on how issues are framed, on how the interests are perceived or misperceived.

Because the conflicts of interest aren't real, the picture of dueling trade blocs is probably all wrong.

If there really were a battle between the U.S., Europe, and Japan for dominance of the industries of the future, each country would need to assemble its allies for that fight. The U.S. would arm itself with a greater NAFTA; Japan would create a ring of trade allies in Asia; Europe would try to incorporate as much of Eastern Europe as it could. But that's not what will actually happen.

Let's start with Asia. There is not now a trading bloc centered on Japan, and there is not likely to be one in the future, for two reasons: China would have to be a large part of that bloc if it is not to be meaningless, and China's economic and political interests would prevent any close alliance with Japan.

Next, turn to Europe. There, a trade bloc already exists; but the idea that Europe is going to become a closer alliance, pursuing a common strategy against the United States and Japan, is becoming less realistic almost daily. European conflicts over Maastricht and monetary policy are only part of the story. There are also conflicts over everything from banana import quotas to the location of vacuum cleaner factories. A grand competitive strategy is not about to come out of this landscape of petty quarrels.

And what about North America? As we all know, NAFTA has been the subject of a lot of impressive rhetoric. At least some of that rhetoric is based on the idea that a unified North American market will give firms based here a competitive advantage in the world at large. That kind of rhetoric has been used extensively, in particular, by U.S. defenders of NAFTA. You've all heard it: "NAFTA will create an economic colossus, a unified $6.2 trillion market." True enough—but the United States alone is already a $5.5 trillion market; Canada adds 0.5, and Mexico is the 0.2. NAFTA will, I hope and believe, happen; but it won't happen as a result of some irresistible move toward trading blocs.

If the world of trading blocs isn't the risk, what is? The answer, I am afraid, is old-fashioned, shabby, self-interested protectionism. What I fear is that the economic difficulties of the advanced countries, together with the breakup of the Washington view in the face of those difficulties, threatens a widespread epidemic of protectionism that will be very bad for developing countries.

Truth and Falsehood in the Conventional Wisdom

At this point it becomes necessary for me to say explicitly what I believe to be true and what I believe to be false in the Washington view.

What is true in the Washington view, at least in broad terms, is the belief in the virtues of free markets and the evils of protectionism. There are qualifications to that view, but they are minor compared with the essential correctness of this position.

What is false in the Washington view, at least as it has come to be interpreted, is the faith in sound money—the dismissal of the usefulness of active monetary policy and of occasional exchange rate realignments. It is not true, in particular, that devaluation is a pointless or ineffective strategy under all circumstances.

Why do I need to say this now? Because it seems all too likely that as the conventional wisdom breaks up, it will be the true parts that will be discarded, while the false ones are retained. If this happens, it will be a bad thing for everyone and a particularly bad thing for developing countries.

Let me give two examples of how I see this bad process happening.

First, consider the mood in Canada. As you all know, Canada already has its free trade agreement with the United States, signed in 1990. That treaty is now, however, extremely unpopular in Canada. Indeed, the man most responsible for that treaty, Brian Mulroney, has resigned as Prime Minister because he knows that his personal unpopularity would mean certain defeat for his party in the next elections. The reason why both the free trade agreement and Mr. Mulroney are so unpopular is the sharp rise in Canadian unemployment and, in particular, the loss of many Canadian manufacturing jobs since 1990.

The shame of it is that Canada's recession and the loss of jobs—indeed, even the loss of competitiveness to the US— have almost nothing to do with the Free Trade Agreement. They are basically the results of a very tight money policy imposed by the Bank of Canada, which is determined to move

Canada all the way to price stability even if the United States is willing to live with a little inflation. The policies of John Crow, who runs the bank, have led to a severe recession and an overvalued Canadian dollar; those are the real causes of distress. But the public doesn't understand that and may, in the end, reject the basically blameless free trade agreement.

A second example: just this week, French voters overwhelmingly rejected the record of the Socialists and gave a huge majority to conservative parties. There is no question that the main issue creating voter unease is the persistence of high and still rising unemployment. And there is also no question that the main reason why France has a recession and is sinking deeper into it is the country's determination to remain pegged to the German mark. If France, like the United Kingdom, were willing to break with the European Monetary System (or better yet, demand a realignment), it would be in an excellent position to engineer, at least, a limited recovery.

Unfortunately, that's not a likely outcome. The rightist parties that have just won the election have made it clear that they are just as committed as the current government to the *franc fort*, the strong franc. So what do they propose? Crude economic nationalism: protectionism for farm products, delaying completion of the Uruguay Round, keeping out goods that Eastern Europe desperately needs to export.

In each of these cases powerful forces have sensed, correctly, that there is something wrong with the conventional wisdom of free markets and sound money. In each case, however, they have thrown out the wrong part, blaming free markets when they should be blaming monetary policy and the exchange rate.

The same thing has not yet happened in the United States, but I have to admit that I am worried. If I try to decide what the shape of the newly emerging conventional wisdom is, it seems to be one that places a totally unjustified weight on the importance of international competition in creating problems for the U.S. economy, both in terms of employment in the short run and growth in the long run. President Clinton's rhetoric on trade issues with Japan and Europe is getting cruder and more belligerent each week. I cannot guarantee that Mexico will be immune.

The Mexican Prospect

Now let me bring all of this home to Mexico. What can we say about the prospects for the Mexican economy, given all that I have been saying?

The first issue to discuss is, of course, NAFTA. Does my questioning of the conventional wisdom imply that NAFTA is a bad idea or that it ought to be reconsidered from either side?

Definitely not. It is certainly true that the NAFTA agreement per se has been oversold, and that—particularly on the U.S. side—the claims for what NAFTA will mean to our economy have been little short of bizarre. Mexico's economy is currently about as big as that of Massachusetts. In terms of direct impact on the United States, the creation of NAFTA is just about as important as the establishment of closer trade relations between the European Community and Sweden as a result of talks between the EC and EFTA. That is, it's not a big thing from the U.S. economic point of view.

Even from a Mexican point of view, NAFTA only extends an already massive process of liberalization. It's a general rule of thumb that the economic costs of protectionism are much more than proportional to the effective rate of protection: a 40 percent rate is 3 or 4 times as harmful as a 20 percent rate. Since Mexico has already removed most of its protection, the remaining gain from moving to free trade will be relatively small. Meanwhile, the United States has pretty low barriers to Mexican exports anyway. So the overall impact, even on Mexico, will be fairly modest.

And yet NAFTA is, in fact, very important because it is a political symbol—a symbol of the durability of Mexico's reforms and of the willingness of the United States to keep its market open to future Mexican exports. If you compare the post-NAFTA trade regime with the current regime, it's not very different. But without NAFTA, the future could see huge backsliding by either or both parties.

And the potential gains from Mexican integration into a wider North American economy *are* large. The conventional wisdom may have ascribed too much miraculous quality to the power of free markets, but it is true that export-oriented industrialization has proved to be a far more effective engine of development than anything else we know. And it would be a terrible thing to let the opportunity for that kind of growth in Mexico go unexploited.

If NAFTA is such a good thing, is there any chance that it will somehow fail to go through? Yes, it could fail—in two ways.

On one side, it is by no means certain that the United States will, in the end, approve NAFTA. I find it hard to believe that we will not; and my best guess will be that the Clinton Administration will push extremely hard for passage, essentially for foreign policy reasons. I think it's obvious, if somewhat offensive, to say that the current government in Mexico is like an American dream: reformist, U.S.-trained technocrats who are willing to drop all the ancient fears of domination and try to produce a modern and eventually democratic nation. The U.S. government would have to be crazy and stupid to threaten in any way the chances of success for that kind of ally. That doesn't mean that it won't happen; but it probably won't.

But there's another kind of way that NAFTA could fail: it could fail in the face of Mexican economic crisis. That crisis might have nothing to do with NAFTA, but neither Canada's nor France's problems have have anything to do with free trade either.

What sort of crisis could happen? Obviously the great risk involves Mexico's current dependence on capital inflows.

As I said earlier, Mexico has, in effect, been given an advance on the presumed future success of its economic reforms, in the form of huge inflows of capital. For the last several years, Mexico has been extraordinarily fashionable among investors and commentators.

Now this has been overdone. I know of one knowledgeable Mexican official who compared the inability of Mexico to borrow before 1990 with the current wave of capital inflows. "We were never that bad," he said, "but we aren't that good either." Even last year it was common to hear Americans (never Mexicans) talk about the Mexican Miracle, as if there had been a China-style takeoff.

Unfortunately, the *real* Mexican miracle is, at best, only nascent. The real growth rate over the last few years has never been more than one or two points above the rate of population growth. There are a few industrial sectors in which near-U.S. productivity has been achieved, but there is no across-the-board surge. Unemployment has continued to rise through the period of resumed economic growth. None of this is news, or a criticism of a government that I deeply admire. The point is simply that Mexico has been the target, not so much of a rational appreciation of its strengths by international investors, as of a sudden irrational financial infatuation.

What if this infatuation ends, as such things do? Or, for that matter, what if growth slows, as it has already begun to do? There is nothing wrong with the basic government strategy of opening up the economy. Indeed, in the long run, that strategy is Mexico's only real hope of escaping from poverty. But there is a looming short- or medium-term problem: unless capital inflows continue at 6 percent of GDP a year, the peso is greatly overvalued.

There is some controversy over whether the very high Mexican real exchange rate today, as compared with 1988, should be regarded as the result of spontaneous inflows of foreign capital or as the result of the attempt to use the exchange rate to control inflation. I don't really think it matters. The real question is whether foreign capital will continue to pour into Mexico at the same rate, which seems unlikely, and what to do if it doesn't.

The conventional wisdom is, of course, that Mexico must stay the course: free markets and sound money. That is what U.S. leaders say now and what they will say right up to the end. I would do the same thing. But those of us who are private citizens have the license to be irresponsible and to say uncomfortable things.

I think that what will happen in Mexico is that here, as in so many other places in the last year, some part of the Washington view will have to be abandoned. There is a possibility that the wrong half will be abandoned, that there will be a reversion to failed protectionist and nationalistic policies. That possibility will be greater if the government sticks to hard money policies until the bitter end.

My guess, however—and I speak as an outsider, with only limited knowledge of Mexican affairs—is that the other half of the equation will give. I have seen absolute assertions of determination to maintain the currency at all costs in Britain and in Sweden; in both cases, logic prevailed in the end, and I think that the countries were actually fortunate that speculators forced their hands. I would be very surprised if sometime soon the same thing does not happen here. In other words, I expect, and welcome, a Mexican devaluation as *part* of the move to complete its economic reform.

10   The Uncomfortable Truth about NAFTA

The debate over the proposed North American Free Trade Agreement has taken on an astonishing salience in American politics. Not since the Smoot-Hawley tariff has trade legislation produced such a bitter polarization of opinion.

The intensity of this debate cannot be understood in terms of the real content or likely consequences of the agreement, nor is the debate's outcome likely to turn on any serious examination of the evidence. It is as hopeless to try to argue with many of NAFTA's opponents as it would have been to try to convince William Jennings Bryan's followers that free silver was not the answer to farmers' problems.

Indeed, the parallel is quite close. The populism of the 1890s represented a desperate attempt to defend agricultural America against deep economic forces that were changing it into an industrial nation. The choice of a monetary standard had very little to do with the real problems of the farm sector; a burst of inflation might have given some highly indebted farmers a brief respite, but it would have done nothing to reverse or even materially slow the industrializing trend.

Reprinted by permission from *Foreign Affairs* (November/December 1993): 13–19. © 1993 by the Council on Foreign Relations, Inc.

Nonetheless, the opposition between free silver and the gold standard was an easily understood symbol—"you shall not crucify this country on a cross of gold" was the nineteenth-century equivalent of a sound bite. And so the almost irrelevant demand for free silver became the core of the populist agenda.

Similarly, the hard-core opposition to NAFTA is rooted in a modern populism that desperately wants to defend industrial America against the forces that are transforming us into a service economy. International trade in general, and trade with Mexico in particular, have very little to do with those forces; clinging to the four percent average tariff the United States currently levies on imports of manufactures from Mexico might save a few low-wage industrial jobs for a little while, but it would do almost nothing to stop or even slow the long-run trends that are the real concern of NAFTA's opponents.

It is an unfortunate fact of politics, however, that bad arguments tend to drive out good. With NAFTA's opponents resorting to simplistic but politically effective rhetoric, the agreement's supporters have responded in kind if not in degree. In the glowing picture now presented by NAFTA advocates inside and outside the administration, the agreement will create hundreds of thousands of high-paying jobs, do wonders for U.S. competitiveness, and assure the prosperity of North America as a whole. This picture is not as grossly false as that painted by NAFTA's opponents, but it does considerably glamorize the reality.

The truth about NAFTA may be summarized in five propositions:

• NAFTA will have no effect on the number of jobs in the United States;

• NAFTA will not hurt and may help the environment;

• NAFTA will, however, produce only a small gain in overall U.S. real income;

• NAFTA will also probably lead to a slight fall in the real wages of unskilled U.S. workers;

• For the United States, NAFTA is essentially a foreign-policy rather than an economic issue.

NAFTA and Jobs

There has been an extensive debate over the prospective job impacts of NAFTA. Some opponents claim that the inflow of imports from, and the outflow of capital to, Mexico will eliminate hundreds of thousands of American jobs. Many supporters, on the other hand, claim that a booming post-NAFTA Mexico will provide a market for sharply increased U.S. exports, adding hundreds of thousands of jobs.[1]

Neither claim is right, nor does the truth lie somewhere in between. Rather, the whole idea of counting jobs gained and lost through trade represents a misunderstanding of the way the U.S. economy works. In particular, it overlooks the fact that other economic policies, especially monetary policy, will almost surely neutralize any potential impact of NAFTA on jobs.

This point seems to be extraordinarily hard to convey to even the sophisticated public. Everyone who thinks about it realizes that the economy is a complex system in which everything affects everything else. Yet people quickly become impatient with the suggestion that one can't understand the likely effects of a change in trade policy without taking into account the probable response of monetary policymakers. Unfortunately, you can't.

Think of the U.S. economy over the next decade as an automobile driving from Boston to New York. Let the average speed of that automobile over the route represent the average level of employment over that decade. And let the dispute over the direct employment effects of NAFTA be represented as an argument over whether there will be a head wind or a tail wind as the car makes its way along the interstate. Then assessing NAFTA's overall job impact is like predicting how the extra wind will affect the car's speed. Job-counting exercises do this by assuming that nothing else changes—in effect, they assume that the engine in our car will receive exactly the same flow of gas that it would have been given in the absence of any wind.

Nobody would think that this was a sensible procedure for predicting automobile speed. After all, cars have drivers, and drivers are not passive—they adjust the flow of gas to achieve a desired speed. I tend to drive interstates at about 63 miles per hour—above the speed limit because I'm always in a hurry, not too far above because I would prefer that the police chase someone else. A five-mile-per-hour head wind or tail wind will not change that average speed; I will simply offset the wind by changing the pressure on my gas pedal.

The U.S. economy also has a driver: the Federal Reserve. Every six weeks or so the Federal Reserve's Open Market Committee meets to decide on a target range for U.S. interest rates. That choice has a far more powerful impact on the unemployment rate than any trade policy. Moreover, it is a choice that responds to economic conditions; the decision to raise or lower interest rates represents a trade-off between the Fed's desire to raise employment (drive somewhere) and its fear of inflation (a speeding ticket). The Fed often miscalculates and ends up with more inflation or less employment than it wanted, but right or wrong the Fed's actions are the most powerful determinants of job growth in America.

Suppose that NAFTA really does lead to a rise in U.S. imports from Mexico, one that would, other things being the same, reduce U.S. employment by 500,000 over the next ten years. Will other things actually be the same? Of course not. The Fed, faced with the prospect of a weaker economy, will set interest rates lower than it otherwise would have. Conversely, other things being equal, if NAFTA would add half a million jobs, interest rates would be higher. The Fed will, without doubt, miss the target—but it is as likely to overshoot as to undershoot, and over the course of a decade there is no reason to suppose that the average level of employment will be any different with NAFTA than without.

This conclusion does not depend on the details of the agreement. If you told me that the direct impact of NAFTA would be a cost to the U.S. economy of five million jobs, perhaps I might worry about whether the Fed would actually have the power to offset this blow, just as I might have trouble driving against gale-force winds. In fact, however, even harsh critics of NAFTA rarely estimate job losses of more than 500,000—less than half of one percent of U.S. employment. The reason the estimates are uniformly small is that anyone who looks at the numbers immediately realizes that U.S. trade barriers against Mexico are already quite low—a four percent tariff on manufactures, higher tariffs on some agricultural products, and a scattering of quantitative restrictions. If Mexico's low wages were the kind of overwhelming attraction to U.S. industry that would generate Ross Perot's "giant sucking sound," those firms would have moved already.

A job loss (or gain) on the order of half of a percent is, however, small change compared with the effects of Federal Reserve policy. Such a change can and will be offset with a change in interest rates of a fraction of a percentage point.

NAFTA and the Environment

Aside from job fears, the most effective argument against NAFTA has been the claim that the agreement will hurt the environment because industry will move south to take advantage of lax Mexican environmental laws and, especially, enforcement of those laws. And there is no question that a Mexican factory typically does more damage to the environment than its U.S. counterpart.

But that is the wrong comparison. Since NAFTA will not lead to a shift of jobs from the United States to Mexico (or vice versa), the relevant question is not whether the Mexican factories that will emerge under NAFTA will be less friendly to the environment than equivalent U.S. plants, but whether they will do more damage than the factories in which Mexican workers would otherwise have been employed.

This is not a question with an obvious answer, but there are at least two reasons to think that on balance NAFTA will be good for Mexico's environment.

One reason is simply that the United States has made the environment an issue, and as a result Mexico will enforce its environmental laws more strictly than it otherwise would have. Despite this fact, Mexican factories will still look pretty bad compared with those in the United States, but that is irrelevant. The point is that they will be cleaner than they would otherwise have been.

A more surprising environmental benefit of NAFTA will be the relocation of Mexican industry. Before 1980 Mexican industrialization, focused on its own domestic market, was largely concentrated in and around Mexico City. Anyone who has been there knows why that presents an environmental problem of literally breathtaking proportions. By contrast, the new export-oriented factories built since Mexico began to follow its new, export-oriented policies are mostly in the north of the country. They may not be models of green production, but at least they are not in the middle of an enclosed valley, a mile above sea level, with 20 million residents.

The Gains from NAFTA

NAFTA will neither create nor destroy jobs, but it will make the existing North American labor force slightly more productive. No serious study—defined as a study by someone whose mind could conceivably have been changed by the evidence—has failed to find that NAFTA will produce a small net gain for the United States. This benefit will come from the usual sources of gains from international trade. First, each country will tend to increase its output in industries in which it is relatively productive, raising the efficiency of the North American economy as a whole. Second, larger markets will allow for better exploitation of economies of scale. Finally, the larger market will lead to greater competition, reducing the inefficiency associated with monopoly power.

The operative word, however, is "small." Few studies indicate that NAFTA could add much more than 0.1 percent to U.S. real income.

Why are the gains so small? First, the United States and Mexico have already moved most of the way to free trade in advance of NAFTA; the agreement does not do all that much more to integrate markets. Second, Mexico's economy is so small—its GDP is less than four percent that of the United States—that for the foreseeable future it will be neither a major supplier nor a major market.

The gains to Mexico from NAFTA are, not surprisingly, much larger as a percentage of that country's national income, if only because the Mexican economy is so much smaller to start with. One recent estimate is representative: it finds that the dollar value of gains from NAFTA will be roughly equally divided between the United States and Mexico (about $6 billion each annually). But this represents a gain of only a little more than 0.1 percent of U.S. GDP, compared with more than 4 percent for Mexico.[2]

NAFTA and Low-wage U.S. Workers

When a country with a highly skilled labor force increases its trade with a country in which skill is at a greater premium, it can expect a decline in the real wages of its own unskilled workers. As a matter of economic principles, we should expect to see at least some adverse impact of NAFTA on the wages of American manual workers.

All the evidence suggests, however, that this effect will be extremely small. For one thing, since the existing barriers to trade between the United States and Mexico are already quite low, it is hard to see how removing them could have any dramatic effect on wage rates.

Moreover, while economic theory suggests that trade between the United States and Mexico should involve an exchange of skill-intensive for labor-intensive products, such a bias in trade against low-wage U.S. workers is surprisingly elusive in the actual trade data. Most notably, the widely cited study of NAFTA by Gary Hufbauer and Jeffrey Schott finds that U.S. industries that compete with imports from Mexico pay almost exactly the same average wage as industries that export to Mexico.

It's worth pointing out that this lack of evidence that trade really does worsen American income distribution is not unique to the Mexican case. Two economists who expected to find a significant effect of trade on wages have concluded that virtually none of the growth in wage inequality in the United States since 1979 is due to international factors. A survey by Lawrence Katz reaches the same conclusion.[3]

As a matter of theory, then, we must concede that NAFTA should be expected to hurt low-skill U.S. workers. In practice, there is no evidence supporting this belief, and the best guess has to be that any such effect will be extremely small.

NAFTA As Foreign Policy

While NAFTA's labor and environmental costs will be minimal, the U.S. public believes otherwise. At the same time, NAFTA's economic benefit to the United States, while real, will be small. One might then ask: Why should the Clinton administration expend a great deal of its depleted political capital in pursuit of an unpopular and economically trivial agreement? The answer is that Mexico's government needs NAFTA, and the United States has a strong interest in helping that government.

Carlos Salinas de Gortari's government is not a model of democratic virtue. From the U.S. point of view, however, it is the best Mexican government in either nation's history. Salinas' market-oriented reformers have done their best to break with a long tradition of anti-American rhetoric. While Mexico has not yet had a truly free presidential election, the trend is clearly toward greater openness and democracy. Not that long ago U.S. intelligence analysts worried that a Mexico hammered by the debt crisis and plunging oil prices might become a radicalized national security nightmare. The friendly neighbor it has instead become is like a State Department dream come true.

But the long-run success of Mexican reform is not guaranteed. Salinas has overseen a radical liberalization of the Mexican economy, above all in international trade. The maximum tariff rate has fallen from 100 percent to 20 percent, the fraction of imports that requires permits has fallen from 93 percent to less than one quarter. These reforms have succeeded in restoring Mexico to the favor of international investors, who have poured huge sums into the Mexican economy since 1990. But the reform has not yet delivered convincing results where it counts: improved living standards among ordinary Mexicans. After eight years of stagnation, in 1990 the Mexican economy began to grow again. The growth, however, has barely kept pace with labor-force expansion. Unemployment remains far higher and real wages far lower than in 1980.

Most economists believe that Mexico's reforms will eventually bear more abundant fruit. In the meantime, however, there is always the risk that either the Mexican populace or the foreign investors who have been supporting the revival of growth will lose faith and patience in the path of reform.

Salinas' decision to seek free trade with the United States should be seen in this context. For his government, NAFTA is a sort of pledge—a pledge to foreign investors that Mexican reform will continue (and that the U.S. market will remain open to goods produced in Mexico). It is also a pledge to the Mexican population that better times are coming.

With the benefit of hindsight, we can see that it might have been better if Salinas had not proposed NAFTA. Perhaps Mexico could have continued down the unilateral path of trade liberalization it has followed since the mid-1980s. This policy would have taken advantage of a U.S. market that was already quite open to Mexican exports of manufactures without stirring up the passions that a formal proposal for free trade has aroused. But it is too late now to reverse course. A rejection of NAFTA by the United States now that the agreement has been negotiated would be a devastating slap in the face to Mexico's reformers.

Nobody can be sure what will happen if NAFTA fails. Perhaps Mexican reform will continue, sadder but wiser. But the most likely forecast is far grimmer: financial crisis for Mexico as investors realize that the success of reform is not guaranteed, political crisis as Mexican populists like Cuauhtémoc Cárdenas Solórzano—who may well have really won the last Presidential election—taunt the leadership with the way America rewards its friends.

If the United States rejects NAFTA, it will virtually be asking for a return to the bad old days of U.S.—Mexican relations. For the United States, this agreement is not about jobs. It is not even about economic efficiency and growth. It is about doing what we can to help a friendly government succeed. It will be a monument to our foolishness if our almost wholly irrational fears about NAFTA end up producing an alienated or even hostile nation on our southern border.

Notes

1. A good summary of the arguments and counterarguments is provided in Gary Hufbauer and Jeffrey Schott, *NAFTA: An Assessment*, Washington, D.C.: Institute for International Economics, 1993.

2. Drusilla K. Brown, Alan V. Deardorff, and Robert M. Stern, "A North American Free Trade Agreement: Analytical Issues and a Computational Assessment," *The World Economy*, January 1992, pp. 15–29.

3. Robert Z. Lawrence and Matthew Slaughter, "Trade and Wages: Giant Sucking Sound or Small Hiccup?" *Brookings Papers on Economic Activity: Microeconomics 1993*, forthcoming; and Lawrence Katz, "Understanding Recent Changes in the Wage Structure," *NBER Reporter*, Winter 1992/93.

11   The Myth of Asia's Miracle

A Cautionary Fable

Once upon a time, Western opinion leaders found themselves both impressed and frightened by the extraordinary growth rates achieved by a set of Eastern economies. Although those economies were still substantially poorer and smaller than those of the West, the speed with which they had transformed themselves from peasant societies into industrial powerhouses, their continuing ability to achieve growth rates several times higher than the advanced nations, and their increasing ability to challenge or even surpass American and European technology in certain areas seemed to call into question the dominance not only of Western power but of Western ideology. The leaders of those nations did not share our faith in free markets or unlimited civil liberties. They asserted with increasing self-confidence that their system was superior: societies that accepted strong, even authoritarian governments and were willing to limit individual liberties in the interest of the common good, take charge of their economies, and sacrifice short-run consumer interests for the sake of long-run growth would

Reprinted by permission from *Foreign Affairs* (November/December 1994): 62–78. © 1994 by the Council on Foreign Relations, Inc.

eventually outperform the increasingly chaotic societies of the
West. And a growing minority of Western intellectuals agreed.

The gap between Western and Eastern economic performance eventually became a political issue. The Democrats
recaptured the White House under the leadership of a young,
energetic new president who pledged to "get the country
moving again"—a pledge that, to him and his closest advisers,
meant accelerating America's economic growth to meet the
Eastern challenge.

The time, of course, was the early 1960s. The dynamic
young president was John F. Kennedy. The technological feats
that so alarmed the West were the launch of Sputnik and the
early Soviet lead in space. And the rapidly growing Eastern
economies were those of the Soviet Union and its satellite
nations.

While the growth of communist economies was the subject
of innumerable alarmist books and polemical articles in the
1950s, some economists who looked seriously at the roots of
that growth were putting together a picture that differed substantially from most popular assumptions. Communist growth
rates were certainly impressive, but not magical. The rapid
growth in output could be fully explained by rapid growth in
inputs: expansion of employment, increases in education levels,
and, above all, massive investment in physical capital. Once
those inputs were taken into account, the growth in output
was unsurprising—or, to put it differently, the big surprise
about Soviet growth was that when closely examined it posed
no mystery.

This economic analysis had two crucial implications. First,
most of the speculation about the superiority of the communist
system—including the popular view that Western economies
could painlessly accelerate their own growth by borrowing
some aspects of that system—was off base. Rapid Soviet economic growth was based entirely on one attribute: the will-

ingness to save, to sacrifice current consumption for the sake of future production. The communist example offered no hint of a free lunch.

Second, the economic analysis of communist countries' growth implied some future limits to their industrial expansion—in other words, implied that a naive projection of their past growth rates into the future was likely to greatly overstate their real prospects. Economic growth that is based on expansion of inputs, rather than on growth in output per unit of input, is inevitably subject to diminishing returns. It was simply not possible for the Soviet economies to sustain the rates of growth of labor force participation, average education levels, and above all the physical capital stock that had prevailed in previous years. Communist growth would predictably slow down, perhaps drastically.

Can there really be any parallel between the growth of Warsaw Pact nations in the 1950s and the spectacular Asian growth that now preoccupies policy intellectuals? At some levels, of course, the parallel is far-fetched: Singapore in the 1990s does not look much like the Soviet Union in the 1950s, and Singapore's Lee Kuan Yew bears little resemblance to the U.S.S.R.'s Nikita Khrushchev and less to Joseph Stalin. Yet the results of recent economic research into the sources of Pacific Rim growth give the few people who recall the great debate over Soviet growth a strong sense of déjà vu. Now, as then, the contrast between popular hype and realistic prospects, between conventional wisdom and hard numbers, remains so great that sensible economic analysis is not only widely ignored, but when it does get aired, it is usually dismissed as grossly implausible.

Popular enthusiasm about Asia's boom deserves to have some cold water thrown on it. Rapid Asian growth is less of a model for the West than many writers claim, and the future prospects for that growth are more limited than almost anyone now imagines. Any such assault on almost universally held beliefs must, of course, overcome a barrier of incredulity. This article began with a disguised account of the Soviet growth debate of 30 years ago to try to gain a hearing for the proposition that we may be revisiting an old error. We have been here before. The problem with this literary device, however, is that so few people now remember how impressive and terrifying the Soviet empire's economic performance once seemed. Before turning to Asian growth, then, it may be useful to review an important but largely forgotten piece of economic history.

"We Will Bury You"

Living in a world strewn with the wreckage of the Soviet empire, it is hard for most people to realize that there was a time when the Soviet economy, far from being a byword for the failure of socialism, was one of the wonders of the world— that when Khrushchev pounded his shoe on the U.N. podium and declared, "We will bury you," it was an economic rather than a military boast. It is therefore a shock to browse through, say, issues of *Foreign Affairs* from the mid-1950s through the early 1960s and discover that at least one article a year dealt with the implications of growing Soviet industrial might.

Illustrative of the tone of discussion was a 1957 article by Calvin B Hoover.[1] Like many Western economists, Hoover criticized official Soviet statistics, arguing that they exaggerated the true growth rate. Nonetheless, he concluded that Soviet claims of astonishing achievement were fully justified: their economy was achieving a rate of growth "twice as high as that attained by any important capitalistic country over any considerable number of years [and] three times as high as the average annual rate of increase in the United States." He concluded that it was probable that "a collectivist, authoritarian state" was inherently better at achieving economic growth than free-market democracies and projected that the Soviet economy might outstrip that of the United States by the early 1970s.

These views were not considered outlandish at the time. On the contrary, the general image of Soviet central planning was that it might be brutal, and might not do a very good job of providing consumer goods, but that it was very effective at promoting industrial growth. In 1960 Wassily Leontief described the Soviet economy as being "directed with determined ruthless skill"—and did so without supporting argument, confident he was expressing a view shared by his readers.

Yet many economists studying Soviet growth were gradually coming to a very different conclusion. Although they did not dispute the fact of past Soviet growth, they offered a new interpretation of the nature of that growth, one that implied a reconsideration of future Soviet prospects. To understand this reinterpretation, it is necessary to make a brief detour into economic theory to discuss a seemingly abstruse, but in fact intensely practical, concept: growth accounting.

Accounting for the Soviet Slowdown

It is a tautology that economic expansion represents the sum of two sources of growth. On one side are increases in "inputs:" growth in employment, in the education level of workers, and in the stock of physical capital (machines, buildings, roads, and so on). On the other side are increases in the output per unit of input; such increases may result from better management or better economic policy, but in the long run are primarily due to increases in knowledge.

The basic idea of growth accounting is to give life to this formula by calculating explicit measures of both. The accounting can then tell us how much of growth is due to each input—say, capital as opposed to labor—and how much is due to increased efficiency.

We all do a primitive form of growth accounting every time we talk about labor productivity; in so doing we are implicitly distinguishing between the part of overall national growth due to the growth in the supply of labor and the part due to an increase in the value of goods produced by the average worker. Increases in labor productivity, however, are not always caused by the increased efficiency of workers. Labor is only one of a number of inputs; workers may produce more, not because they are better managed or have more technological knowledge, but simply because they have better machinery. A man with a bulldozer can dig a ditch faster than one with only a shovel, but he is not more efficient; he just has more capital to work with. The aim of growth accounting is to produce an index that combines all measurable inputs and to measure the rate of growth of national income relative to that index—to estimate what is known as "total factor productivity."[2]

So far this may seem like a purely academic exercise. As soon as one starts to think in terms of growth accounting, however, one arrives at a crucial insight about the process of economic growth: sustained growth in a nation's per capita income can only occur if there is a rise in output *per unit of input*.[3]

Mere increases in inputs, without an increase in the efficiency with which those inputs are used—investing in more machinery and infrastructure—must run into diminishing returns; input-driven growth is inevitably limited.

How, then, have today's advanced nations been able to achieve sustained growth in per capita income over the past 150 years? The answer is that technological advances have led to a continual increase in total factor productivity—a continual rise in national income for each unit of input. In a famous

estimate, MIT Professor Robert Solow concluded that technological progress has accounted for 80 percent of the long-term
rise in U.S. per capita income, with increased investment in
capital explaining only the remaining 20 percent.

When economists began to study the growth of the Soviet
economy, they did so using the tools of growth accounting. Of
course, Soviet data posed some problems. Not only was it
hard to piece together usable estimates of output and input
(Raymond Powell, a Yale professor, wrote that the job "in
many ways resembled an archaeological dig"), but there were
philosophical difficulties as well. In a socialist economy one
could hardly measure capital input using market returns, so
researchers were forced to impute returns based on those in
market economies at similar levels of development. Still, when
the efforts began, researchers were pretty sure about what they
would find. Just as capitalist growth had been based on growth
in both inputs and efficiency, with efficiency the main source
of rising per capita income, they expected to find that rapid
Soviet growth reflected both rapid input growth and rapid
growth in efficiency.

But what they actually found was that Soviet growth was
based on rapid growth in inputs—end of story. The rate of
efficiency growth was not only unspectacular, it was well below the rates achieved in Western economies. Indeed, by some
estimates, it was virtually nonexistent.[4]

The immense Soviet efforts to mobilize economic resources
were hardly news. Stalinist planners had moved millions of
workers from farms to cities, pushed millions of women into
the labor force and millions of men into longer hours, pursued
massive programs of education, and above all plowed an ever-
growing proportion of the country's industrial output back into
the construction of new factories. Still, the big surprise was
that once one had taken the effects of these more or less

measurable inputs into account, there was nothing left to explain. The most shocking thing about Soviet growth was its comprehensibility.

This comprehensibility implied two crucial conclusions. First, claims about the superiority of planned over market economies turned out to be based on a misapprehension. If the Soviet economy had a special strength, it was its ability to mobilize resources, not its ability to use them efficiently. It was obvious to everyone that the Soviet Union in 1960 was much less efficient than the United States. The surprise was that it showed no signs of closing the gap.

Second, because input-driven growth is an inherently limited process, Soviet growth was virtually certain to slow down. Long before the slowing of Soviet growth became obvious, it was predicted on the basis of growth accounting. (Economists did not predict the implosion of the Soviet economy a generation later, but that is a whole different problem.)

Its an interesting story and a useful cautionary tale about the dangers of naive extrapolation of past trends. But is it relevant to the modern world?

Paper Tigers

A first, it is hard to see anything in common between the Asian success stories of recent years and the Soviet Union of three decades ago. Indeed, it is safe to say that the typical business traveler to, say, Singapore, ensconced in one of that city's gleaming hotels, never even thinks of any parallel to its roach-infested counterparts in Moscow. How can the slick exuberance of the Asian boom be compared with the Soviet Union's grim drive to industrialize?

And yet there are surprising similarities. The newly industrializing countries of Asia, like the Soviet Union of the 1950s,

have achieved rapid growth in large part through an astonishing mobilization of resources. Once one accounts for the
role of rapidly growing inputs in these countries' growth, one
finds little left to explain. Asian growth, like that of the Soviet
Union in its high-growth era, seems to be driven by extraordinary growth in inputs like labor and capital rather than by
gains in efficiency.[5]

Consider, in particular, the case of Singapore. Between 1966
and 1990, the Singaporean economy grew a remarkable 8.5
percent per annum, three times as fast as the United States; per
capita income grew at a 6.6 percent rate, roughly doubling
every decade. This achievement seems to be a kind of economic miracle. But the miracle turns out to have been based on
perspiration rather than inspiration: Singapore grew through a
mobilization of resources that would have done Stalin proud.
The employed share of the population surged from 27 to 51
percent. The educational standards of that work force were
dramatically upgraded: while in 1966 more than half the workers had no formal education at all, by 1990 two-thirds had
completed secondary education. Above all, the country had
made an awesome investment in physical capital: investment as
a share of output rose from 11 to more than 40 percent.[6]

Even without going through the formal exercise of growth
accounting, these numbers should make it obvious that Singapore's growth has been based largely on one-time changes in
behavior that cannot be repeated. Over the past generation the
percentage of people employed has almost doubled; it cannot
double again. A half-educated work force has been replaced by
one in which the bulk of workers has high school diplomas; it is
unlikely that a generation from now most Singaporeans will
have Ph.D.s. And an investment share of 40 percent is amaz-
ingly high by any standard; a share of 70 percent would be
ridiculous. So one can immediately conclude that Singapore is

unlikely to achieve future growth rates comparable to those of the past.

But it is only when one actually does the quantitative accounting that the astonishing result emerges: all of Singapore's growth can be explained by increases in measured inputs. There is no sign at all of increased efficiency. In this sense, the growth of Lee Kuan Yew's Singapore is an economic twin of the growth of Stalin's Soviet Union—growth achieved purely through mobilization of resources. Of course, Singapore today is far more prosperous than the U.S.S.R. ever was—even at its peak in the Brezhnev years—because Singapore is closer to, though still below, the efficiency of Western economies. The point, however, is that Singapore's economy has always been relatively efficient; it just used to be starved of capital and educated workers.

Singapore's case is admittedly the most extreme. Other rapidly growing East Asian economies have not increased their labor force participation as much, made such dramatic improvements in educational levels, or raised investment rates quite as far. Nonetheless, the basic conclusion is the same: there is startlingly little evidence of improvements in efficiency. Kim and Lau conclude of the four Asian "tigers" that "the hypothesis that there has been no technical progress during the postwar period cannot be rejected for the four East Asian newly industrialized countries." Young, more poetically, notes that once one allows for their rapid growth of inputs, the productivity performance of the "tigers" falls "from the heights of Olympus to the plains of Thessaly."

This conclusion runs so counter to conventional wisdom that it is extremely difficult for the economists who have reached it to get a hearing. As early as 1982 a Harvard graduate student, Yuan Tsao, found little evidence of efficiency growth in her dissertation on Singapore, but her work was, as

Young puts it, "ignored or dismissed as unbelievable." When Kim and Lau presented their work at a 1992 conference in Taipei, it received a more respectful hearing, but had little immediate impact. But when Young tried to make the case for input-driven Asian growth at the 1993 meetings of the European Economic Association, he was met with a stone wall of disbelief.

In Young's most recent paper there is an evident tone of exasperation with this insistence on clinging to the conventional wisdom in the teeth of the evidence. He titles the paper "The Tyranny of Numbers"—by which he means that you may not want to believe this, buster, but there's just no way around the data. He begins with an ironic introduction, written in a deadpan, Sergeant Friday, "Just the facts, ma'am" style: "This is a fairly boring and tedious paper, and is intentionally so. This paper provides no new interpretations of the East Asian experience to interest the historian, derives no new theoretical implications of the forces behind the East Asian growth process to motivate the theorist, and draws no new policy implications from the subtleties of East Asian government intervention to excite the policy activist. Instead, this paper concentrates its energies on providing a careful analysis of the historical patterns of output growth, factor accumulation, and productivity growth in the newly industrializing countries of East Asia."

Of course, he is being disingenuous. His conclusion undermines most of the conventional wisdom about the future role of Asian nations in the world economy and, as a consequence, in international politics. But readers will have noticed that the statistical analysis that puts such a different interpretation on Asian growth focuses on the "tigers," the relatively small countries to whom the name "newly industrializing countries" was first applied. But what about the large countries? What about Japan and China?

The Great Japanese Growth Slowdown

Many people who are committed to the view that the destiny of the world economy lies with the Pacific Rim are likely to counter skepticism about East Asian growth prospects with the example of Japan. Here, after all, is a country that started out poor and has now become the second-largest industrial power. Why doubt that other Asian nations can do the same?

There are two answers to that question. First, while many authors have written of an "Asian system"—a common denominator that underlies all of the Asian success stories—the statistical evidence tells a different story. Japan's growth in the 1950s and 1960s does not resemble Singapore's growth in the 1970s and 1980s. Japan, unlike the East Asian "tigers," seems to have grown both through high rates of input growth and through high rates of efficiency growth. Today's fast-growth economies are nowhere near converging on U.S. efficiency levels, but Japan is staging an unmistakable technological catch-up.

Second, while Japan's historical performance has indeed been remarkable, the era of miraculous Japanese growth now lies well in the past. Most years Japan still manages to grow faster than the other advanced nations, but that gap in growth rates is now far smaller than it used to be, and is shrinking.

The story of the great Japanese growth slowdown has been oddly absent from the vast polemical literature on Japan and its role in the world economy. Much of that literature seems stuck in a time warp, with authors writing as if Japan were still the miracle growth economy of the 1960s and early 1970s. Granted, the severe recession that has gripped Japan since

1991 will end soon if it has not done so already, and the Japanese economy will probably stage a vigorous short-term recovery. The point, however, is that even a full recovery will only reach a level that is far below what many sensible observers predicted 20 years ago.

It may be useful to compare Japan's growth prospects as they appeared 20 years ago and as they appear now. In 1973 Japan was still a substantially smaller and poorer economy than the United States. Its per capita GDP was only 55 percent of America's, while its overall GDP was only 27 percent as large. But the rapid growth of the Japanese economy clearly portended a dramatic change. Over the previous decade Japan's real GDP had grown at a torrid 8.9 percent annually, with per capita output growing at a 7.7 percent rate. Although American growth had been high by its own historical standards, at 3.9 percent (2.7 percent per capita) it was not in the same league. Clearly, the Japanese were rapidly gaining on us.

In fact, a straightforward projection of these trends implied that a major reversal of positions lay not far in the future. At the growth rate of 1963–73, Japan would overtake the United States in real per capita income by 1985, and total Japanese output would exceed that of the United States by 1998! At the time, people took such trend projections very seriously indeed. One need only look at the titles of such influential books as Herman Kahn's *The Emerging Japanese Superstate* or Ezra Vogel's *Japan as Number One* to remember that Japan appeared, to many observers, to be well on its way to global economic dominance.

Well, it has not happened, at least not so far. Japan has indeed continued to rise in the economic rankings, but at a far more modest pace than those projections suggested. In 1992 Japan's per capita income was still only 83 percent of the United States', and its overall output was only 42 percent of the American level. The reason was that growth from 1973 to 1992 was far slower than in the high-growth years: GDP grew only 3.7 percent annually, and GDP per capita grew only 3 percent per year. The United States also experienced a growth slowdown after 1973, but it was not nearly as drastic.

If one projects those post-1973 growth rates into the future, one still sees a relative Japanese rise, but a far less dramatic one. Following 1973–92 trends, Japan's per capita income will outstrip that of the United States in 2002; its overall output does not exceed America's until the year 2047. Even this probably overestimates Japanese prospects. Japanese economists generally believe that their country's rate of growth of potential output, the rate that it will be able to sustain once it has taken up the slack left by the recession, is now no more than three percent. And that rate is achieved only through a very high rate of investment, nearly twice as high a share of GDP as in the United States. When one takes into account the growing evidence for at least a modest acceleration of U.S. productivity growth in the last few years, one ends up with the probable conclusion that Japanese efficiency is gaining on that of the United States at a snail's pace, if at all, and there is the distinct possibility that per capita income in Japan may never overtake that in America. In other words, Japan is not quite as overwhelming an example of economic prowess as is sometimes thought, and in any case Japan's experience has much less in common with that of other Asian nations than is generally imagined.

The China Syndrome

For the skeptic, the case of China poses much greater difficulties about Asian destiny than that of Japan. Although China is still a very poor country, its population is so huge that it will become a major economic power if it achieves even a fraction of Western productivity levels. And China, unlike Japan, has in recent years posted truly impressive rates of economic growth. What about its future prospects?

Accounting for China's boom is difficult for both practical and philosophical reasons. The practical problem is that while we know that China is growing very rapidly, the quality of the numbers is extremely poor. It was recently revealed that official Chinese statistics on foreign investment have been overstated by as much as a factor of six. The reason was that the government offers tax and regulatory incentives to foreign investors, providing an incentive for domestic entrepreneurs to invent fictitious foreign partners or to work through foreign fronts. This episode hardly inspires confidence in any other statistic that emanates from that dynamic but awesomely corrupt society.

The philosophical problem is that it is unclear what year to use as a baseline. If one measures Chinese growth from the point at which it made a decisive turn toward the market, say 1978, there is little question that there has been dramatic improvement in efficiency as well as rapid growth in inputs. But it is hardly surprising that a major recovery in economic efficiency occurred as the country emerged from the chaos of Mao Zedong's later years. If one instead measures growth from before the Cultural Revolution, say 1964, the picture looks more like the East Asian "tigers:" only modest growth in efficiency, with most growth driven by inputs. This calculation, however, also seems unfair: one is weighing down the buoyant performance of Chinese capitalism with the leaden performance of Chinese socialism. Perhaps we should simply split the difference: guess that some, but not all, of the efficiency gains since the turn toward the market represent a one-time recovery, while the rest represent a sustainable trend.

Even a modest slowing in China's growth will change the geopolitical outlook substantially. The World Bank estimates that the Chinese economy is currently about 40 percent as large as that of the United States. Suppose that the U.S. economy continues to grow at 2.5 percent each year. If China can continue to grow at 10 percent annually, by the year 2010 its economy will be a third larger than ours. But if Chinese growth is only a more realistic 7 percent, its GDP will be only 82 percent of that of the United States. There will still be a substantial shift of the world's economic center of gravity, but it will be far less drastic than many people now imagine.

The Mystery That Wasn't

The extraordinary record of economic growth in the newly industrializing countries of East Asia has powerfully influenced the conventional wisdom about both economic policy and geopolitics. Many, perhaps most, writers on the global economy now take it for granted that the success of these economies demonstrates three propositions. First, there is a major diffusion of world technology in progress, and Western nations are losing their traditional advantage. Second, the world's economic center of gravity will inevitably shift to the Asian nations of the western Pacific. Third, in what is perhaps a minority view, Asian successes demonstrate the superiority of economies with fewer civil liberties and more planning than we in the West have been willing to accept.

All three conclusions are called into question by the simple observation that the remarkable record of East Asian growth has been matched by input growth so rapid that Asian economic growth, incredibly, ceases to be a mystery.

Consider first the assertion that the advanced countries are losing their technological advantage. A heavy majority of recent tracts on the world economy have taken it as self-evident that technology now increasingly flows across borders, and that newly industrializing nations are increasingly able to match the productivity of more established economies. Many writers warn that this diffusion of technology will place huge strains on Western society as capital flows to the Third World and imports from those nations undermine the West's industrial base.

There are severe conceptual problems with this scenario even if its initial premise is right.[7] But in any case, while technology may have diffused within particular industries, the available evidence provides absolutely no justification for the view that overall world technological gaps are vanishing. On the contrary, Kim and Lau find "no apparent convergence between the technologies" of the newly industrialized nations and the established industrial powers; Young finds that the rates in the growth of efficiency in the East Asian "tigers" are no higher than those in many advanced nations.

The absence of any dramatic convergence in technology helps explain what would otherwise be a puzzle: in spite of a great deal of rhetoric about North-South capital movement, actual capital flows to developing countries in the 1990s have so far been very small—and they have primarily gone to Latin America, not East Asia. Indeed, several of the East Asian "tigers" have recently become significant exporters of capital. This behavior would be extremely odd if these economies, which still pay wages well below advanced-country levels, were rapidly achieving advanced-country productivity. It is, however, perfectly reasonable if growth in East Asia has been primarily input-driven, and if the capital piling up there is beginning to yield diminishing returns.

If growth in East Asia is indeed running into diminishing returns, however, the conventional wisdom about an Asian-centered world economy needs some rethinking. It would be a mistake to overstate this case: barring a catastrophic political upheaval, it is likely that growth in East Asia will continue to outpace growth in the West for the next decade and beyond. But it will not do so at the pace of recent years. From the perspective of the year 2010, current projections of Asian supremacy extrapolated from recent trends may well look almost as silly as 1960s-vintage forecasts of Soviet industrial supremacy did from the perspective of the Brezhnev years.

Finally, the realities of East Asian growth suggest that we may have to unlearn some popular lessons. It has become common to assert that East Asian economic success demonstrates the fallacy of our traditional laissez-faire approach to economic policy and that the growth of these economies shows the effectiveness of sophisticated industrial policies and selective protectionism. Authors such as James Fallows have asserted that the nations of that region have evolved a common "Asian system," whose lessons we ignore at our peril. The extremely diverse institutions and policies of the various newly industrialized Asian countries, let alone Japan, cannot really be called a common system. But in any case, if Asian success reflects the benefits of strategic trade and industrial policies, those benefits should surely be manifested in an unusual and impressive rate of growth in the efficiency of the economy. And there is no sign of such exceptional efficiency growth.

The newly industrializing countries of the Pacific Rim have received a reward for their extraordinary mobilization of resources that is no more than what the most boringly conventional economic theory would lead us to expect. If there is a secret to Asian growth, it is simply deferred gratification, the willingness to sacrifice current satisfaction for future gain.

That's a hard answer to accept, especially for those American policy intellectuals who recoil from the dreary task of reducing deficits and raising the national savings rate. But economics is not a dismal science because the economists like it that way; it is because in the end we must submit to the tyranny not just of the numbers, but of the logic they express.

Notes

1. Hoover's tone—critical of Soviet data but nonetheless accepting the fact of extraodinary achievement—was typical of much of the commentary of the time (see, for example, a series of articles in *The Atlantic Monthly* by Edward Crankshaw, beginning with "Soviet Industry" in the November 1955 issue). Anxiety about the political implications of Soviet growth reached its high-water mark in 1959, the year Khrushchev visited America. *Newsweek* took Khrushchev's boasts seriously enough to warn that the Soviet Union might well be "on the high road to economic domination of the world." And in hearings held by the Joint Economic Committee late that year, CIA Director Allen Dulles warned, "If the Soviet industrial growth rate persists at eight or nine percent per annum over the next decade, as is forecast, the gap between our two economies...will be dangerously narrowed."

2. At first, creating an index of all inputs may seem like comparing apples and oranges, that is, trying to add together noncomparable items like the hours a worker puts in and the cost of the new machine he uses. How does one determine the weights for the different components? The economists' answer is to use market returns. If the average worker earns $15 an hour, give each person-hour in the index a weight of $15; if a machine that costs $100,000 on average earns $10,000 in profits each year (a 10 percent rate of return), then give each such machine a weight of $10,000; and so on.

3. To see why, let's consider a hypothetical example. To keep matters simple, let's assume that the country has a stationary population and labor forces, so that all increases in the investment in machinery, etc., raise the amount of capital per worker in the country. Let us finally make up some arbitrary numbers. Specifically, let us assume that initially each worker is equipped with $10,000 worth of equipment; that each worker produces goods and services worth

$10,000; and that capital initially earns a 40 percent rate of return, that is, each $10,000 of machinery earns annual profits of $4,000.

Suppose, now, that this country consistently invests 20 percent of its output, that is, uses 20 percent of its income to add to its capital stock. How rapidly will the economy grow?

Initially, very fast indeed. In the first year, the capital stock per worker will rise by 20 percent of $10,000, that is, by $20,000. At a 40 percent rate of return, that will increase output by $800: an 8 percent rate of growth.

But this high rate of growth will not be sustainable. Consider the situation of the economy by the time that capital per worker has doubled to $20,000. First, output per worker will not have increased in the same proportion, because capital stock is only one input. Even with the additions to capital stock up to that point achieving a 40 percent rate of return, output per worker will have increased only to $14,000. And the rate of return is also certain to decline—say to 30 or even 25 percent. (One bulldozer added to a construction project can make a huge difference to productivity. By the time a dozen are on-site, one more may not make that much difference.) The combination of those factors means that if the investment share of output is the same, the growth rate will sharply decline. Taking 20 percent of $14,000 gives us $2,800; at a 30 percent rate of return, this will raise output by only $840, that is, generate a growth rate of only 6 percent; at a 25 percent rate of return it will generate a growth rate of only 5 percent. As capital continues to accumulate, the rate of return and hence the rate of growth will continue to decline.

4. This work was summarized by Raymond Powell, "Economic Growth in the U.S.S.R.," *Scientific American*, December 1968.

5. There have been a number of recent efforts to quantify the sources of rapid growth in the Pacific Rim. Key readings include two papers by Professor Lawrence Lau of Stanford University and his associate Jong-Il Kim, "The Sources of the Growth of the East Asian Newly Industralized Countries," *Journal of the Japanese and International Economies*, 1994, and "The Role of Human Capital in the Economic Growth of the East Asian Newly Industrialized Countries," mimeo, Stanford University, 1993; and three papers by Professor Alwyn Young, a rising star in growth economics, "A Tale of Two Cities: Factor Accumulation and Technical Change in Hong Kong and Singa-

pore," *NBER Macroeconomics Annual 1992*. MIT Press, "Lessons from the East Asian NICS: A Contrarian View," *European Economic Review Papers and Proceedings*, May 1994; and "The Tyranny of Numbers: Confronting the Statistical Realities of the East Asian Growth Experience," NBER Working Paper No. 4680, March 1994.

6. These figures are taken from Young, *ibid*. Although foreign corporations have played an important role in Singapore's economy, the great bulk of investment in Singapore, as in all of the newly industralized East Asian economies, has been financed out of domestic savings.

7. See Paul Krugman, "Does Third World Growth Hurt First World Prosperity?" *Harvard Business Review*, July 1994.

IV   Technology and Society

12   Technology's Revenge

In his science-fiction novel of 1952, *Player Piano*, Kurt Vonnegut imagined a future in which the ingenuity of engineers has allowed machines to eliminate virtually all manual labor. The social consequences of this technological creativity, in his vision, are disastrous: Most people, instead of finding gainful employment, live on the dole or are employed in pointless government make-work programs. Only the most creative and talented can find meaningful work, and their numbers steadily shrink as more and more jobs are automated out of existence.

For the first 20 years after *Player Piano* appeared, it seemed that Vonnegut could not have been more wrong. Between World War II and the early 1970s, the world's advanced economies were spectacularly successful at creating precisely the kind of employment that he imagined automation would destroy: well-paying jobs for workers of average skills and education. Social observers waxed eloquent over the unprecedented prosperity of the working class. Thanks to the 30-year "Go-Getter Bourgeois business boom," writer Tom Wolfe announced, "the word *proletarian* can no longer be used in this country with a straight face." Economists, who had always

Reprinted by permission from *The Wilson Quarterly* (Autumn 1994): 56–64.

regarded most fears about automation as nonsense, felt confirmed in their dismissal of the issue.

But the past 20 years have not been good ones for ordinary workers. Even as the earnings of many college-educated workers soared in the United States, young men without college degrees have seen their real wages drop by 20 percent or more—this in spite of productivity growth which, while disappointing, nonetheless allowed the average American worker to produce about 25 percent more in 1993 than in 1973. In Europe, the growth of wage inequality has been less dramatic, but there has been a steady, seemingly inexorable rise in unemployment, from less than three percent in 1973 to more than 11 percent today (versus six percent in the United States).

Many economists believe that the American and European experiences are two sides of the same coin. For whatever reason, employers have been increasingly reluctant to pay for the services of those who do not offer something exceptional. In the United States, where unemployment benefits are relatively skimpy and of relatively short duration (26 weeks), and where the unemployed often find themselves without health insurance, workers have little choice but to accept jobs no matter how low the pay. Thus, U.S. labor markets have been, in the fine euphemism of official documents, "flexible." In Europe, much more generous social benefits make it easier for workers to turn down jobs they find unacceptable, and various government regulations and restrictions make employers less willing and able to offer low-wage jobs in any case. Thus, the same forces that lead to less pay for the less skilled in the United States lead to rising unemployment for the same group in Europe. The larger outcome is the same on both sides of the Atlantic: The broad equality of economic outcomes that the postwar West had come to take for granted seems to be receding into memory.

Most people who read intellectual magazines or watch public television know why this is happening. Growing international competition, especially from low-wage countries, is destroying the good manufacturing jobs that used to be the backbone of the working class. Unfortunately, what these people "know" happens to be flatly untrue. The real reason for rising wage inequality is subtler: Technological change since 1970 has increased the premium paid to highly skilled workers, from data processing specialists to physicians. The big question, of course, is whether this trend will continue.

Before we can get to that question, however, it is necessary to clear away some of the underbrush. Much public discussion of jobs—even among people who consider themselves sophisticated and well-informed—has been marked by basic misunderstandings of the facts. Consider this statement: "Modern technologies of transportation and communication make it possible to produce anything anywhere. This technological shrinking of the world has only been reinforced by the fall of communism, which has made the Third World safe for multinational corporations. As a result, a massive redeployment of capital and technology from the high-wage countries of the West to low-wage developing nations is now occurring. This redeployment of capital along with the flood of low-cost imports is destroying the well-paying manufacturing jobs that used to support a large middle class in the United States and Europe. In short, globalization favors Western capital, but it is devastating to Western labor."

Convincing as this may sound, the statement is specious. In fact, I made it up to illustrate a view of the world that passes for sophistication among many policy intellectuals but is almost completely refuted by the available evidence.[1]

At the basic level, this conventional view suggests that capital and technology are in fixed supply, and that growth in new countries necessarily comes at the expense of the more established countries. The reality is that the diffusion of technology, while it increases competition faced by the leaders' exports, also expands their markets and reduces the price of their imports. For example, the United States must buy virtually all of its laptop computers from foreign producers, but the growth of overseas production has enlarged markets for U.S.-made microprocessors and cut the price of laptops. In principle, the net result of the diffusion of technology could be either to raise or to lower First World income. In practice, there is little discernible effect.

Nor is the world supply of capital a fixed quantity. As countries grow, they also save—in the case of rapidly growing Asian nations, they save at astonishing rates. Third World growth may thus add to the world supply of capital as fast as or faster than it increases the demand.

Moreover, the amount of imports arriving from newly industrializing countries and the size of capital flows going to them fall far short of what is suggested in alarmist rhetoric. If there is a single piece of knowledge that separates serious international economists from fashionable popularizers, it is a sense of *how big* the world economy really is. We have all heard enough stories of particular factories that have moved to Mexico or Indonesia to form the impression that a massive global trend is underway. But even a billion-dollar investment is insignificant amid the sheer immensity of the economies of the industrialized nations. Their combined gross domestic products in 1990 exceeded $19 *trillion*, and their combined domestic investment exceeded $4 trillion. The total movement of capital to newly industrializing countries in 1993—a record year, unlikely to be surpassed in 1994—was roughly $100

billion. That is, less than 2.5 percent of the investment of the
First World actually flowed south. While it is true that tens or
even hundreds of thousands of workers in advanced countries
have lost their jobs to low-wage imports, the total labor force
in the industrialized world is more than 400 million strong;
almost every effort to quantify the reasons why more than 30
million of these workers do not have jobs finds that Third
World competition plays little if any role. That is not to say
that international trade and capital mobility could not have a
more important impact in the future. But declining wages and
rising unemployment are not things that might happen once
globalization really gets going; they are trends that have been
in progress for 20 years. What is causing them?

Economists use the word "technology" somewhat differently
from normal people. *Webster's* defines technology as "applied
science," which is pretty much the normal usage. When economists speak of technological change, however, they mean any
kind of change in the relationship between inputs and outputs.
If, for example, a manufacturer discovers that "empowering"
workers by giving them a voice in how the factory is run
improves quality—and allows the plant to employ fewer
supervisors—then in the economic sense this would be an
improvement in the technology, one that is biased against
employment of managers. If, however, a manufacturer discovers that workers will produce more when there are many
supervisors constantly checking on them, this is also a technological improvement, albeit one biased *toward* employment of
managers.

In this economist's sense, it seems undeniable that over the
past 20 years the advanced nations have experienced technological change that is strongly biased in favor of skilled
workers. The evidence is straightforward. The wages of skilled

Table 12.1
America's fastest growing occupations, 1992–2005
(In parentheses: the number of projected new jobs, in thousands)

	Percent change
Home health aides (479)	138
Human services workers (256)	136
Personal and home care aides (166)	130
Computer engineers and scientists (236)	112
Systems analysts (501)	110
Physical and Corrective therapy assistants and aides (57)	93
Physical therapists (79)	88
Paralegals (81)	86
Teachers, special education (267)	74
Medical assistants (128)	71
Detectives, private (41)	70
Correction officers (197)	70
Child care workers (450)	66
Travel agents (76)	66
Radiologic technologists and technicians (102)	63
Nursery workers (44)	62
Medical records technicians (47)	61
Operations research analysts (27)	61
Occupational therapists (24)	60
Legal secretaries (160)	57
Teachers, preschool and kindergarten (236)	54
Manicurists (19)	54
Producers, directors, actors, and entertainers (69)	54
Speech-language pathologists and audiologists (37)	51
Flight attendants (47)	51
Guards (408)	51

Source: U.S. Bureau of Labor Statistics
Note: The fastest growing occupations in percentage terms are not necessarily those that will produce the largest number of new jobs. The most growth in absolute terms will occur in the retail sales clerk category, which will grow by 786,000 jobs (21 percent) between 1992 and 2005.

workers, from technicians to corporate executives, have risen sharply relative to the wages of the less skilled. In 1979, a young man with a college degree and five years on the job earned only 30 percent more than one with similar experience and a high school degree; by 1989, the premium had jumped to 74 percent. If the technology of the economy had not changed, this sharp increase in the relative cost of skilled workers would have given employers a strong incentive to cut back and substitute less-skilled workers where they could. In fact, exactly the opposite happened: Across the board, employers *raised* the average skill level of their work forces.

It is hard not to conclude that this technologically driven shift in demand has been a key cause of the growth of earnings inequality in the United States as well as much of the rise in unemployment in Europe. It is not the only possible explanation. It could have been the case that rising demand for skilled workers was not so much the result of greater demand for skill within each industry as of a shift in the mix of industries toward those sectors that employ a high ratio of skilled to unskilled workers. That sort of shift could, for example, be the result of increased trade with labor-abundant Third World countries. But in fact the overwhelming evidence is that the demand for unskilled workers has fallen not because of a change in *what* we produce but because of a change in *how* we produce.

Is it really possible for technological progress to harm large numbers of people? It is and it has been. Economic historians confirm what readers of Charles Dickens already knew, that the unprecedented technological progress of the Industrial Revolution took a long time to be reflected in higher real wages for most workers. Why? A likely answer is that early industrial technology was not only labor saving but strongly capital using—that is, the new technology encouraged industrialists to use less labor and to invest more capital to produce a given amount of output. The result was a fall in the demand for labor that kept real wages stagnant for perhaps 50 years, even as the incomes of England's propertied classes soared.

Economists more or less agree that the same thing is happening to the Western world today, except that the benefits of biased technological change are flowing not to capital but to the highly skilled.

It is easy to understand why the Industrial Revolution was capital using and labor saving. Just think of a factory full of power looms replacing thousands of hand weavers—the development that gave rise to the Luddite rebellion in early-19th-century Britain. Can we come up with comparable images that relate recent technological change in the economist's sense to its more normal usage? That is, what is changing in the way that we produce goods and service that has apparently devalued less-skilled workers?

The short answer is that we do not know. There are, however, several interesting stories and pieces of evidence.

Probably the simplest story about how modern technology may promote inequality is that the rapid spread of computers favors those who possess the knowledge needed to use them effectively. Anecdotes are easy to offer. Economist Jagdish Bhagwati cites the "computer with a single skilled operator that replaces half a dozen unskilled typists." Anecdotes are no substitute for real quantitative evidence, but for what it is worth, serious studies by labor economists do suggest that growing computer use can explain as much as one-half of the increase in the earnings edge enjoyed by college graduates during the 1980s.

Yet there is probably more to the story. The professions that have seen the largest increases in incomes since the 1970s have been in fields whose practitioners are not obviously placed in greater demand by computers: lawyers, doctors, and, above all, corporate executives. And the growth of inequality in the United States has a striking "fractal" quality: Widening gaps *between* education levels and professions are mirrored by increased inequality of earnings *within* professions. Lawyers make much more compared with janitors than they did 15 years ago, but the best-paid lawyers also make much more compared with the average lawyer. Again, this is hard to reconcile with a simple story in which new computers require people who know how to use them.

One intriguing hypothesis about the relationship between technology and income distribution, a hypothesis that can explain why people who do not operate computers or fax machines can nonetheless be enriched by them at the expense of others, is the "superstar" hypothesis of Sherwin Rosen, an economist at the University of Chicago. Almost 15 years ago, before the explosion of inequality had become apparent, Rosen argued in the *Journal of Political Economy* that communication and information technology extend an individual's span of influence and control. A performance by a stage actor can be watched by only a few hundred people, while one by a television star can be watched by tens of millions. Less obviously, an executive, a lawyer, or even an entrepreneurial academic can use computers, faxes, and electronic mail to keep a finger in far more pies than used to be possible. As a result, Rosen predicted, the wage structure would increasingly come to have a "tournament" quality: A few people, those judged by whatever criteria to be the best, would receive huge financial rewards, while those who were merely competent would receive little. The point of Rosen's analysis was that technology may not so much directly substitute for workers as multiply the power of particular individuals, allowing these lucky tournament winners to substitute for large numbers of the less fortunate. Television does not take the place of hundreds of struggling standup nightclub comedians; it allows Jay Leno to take their place instead.

Will technology continue to favor a few lucky people over the rest, or will the last quarter of the 20th century turn out to have been a transitory bad patch for the common man? At first sight, it seems obvious that the progress of technology must lead to an ever-growing premium on skill. How could it be otherwise in an era when sophisticated computers and information systems are becoming ever more crucial to our economy? Isn't it obvious that the only good jobs will be for those who possess exceptional intellectual talent and skills—those who, in the phrase of Secretary of Labor Robert Reich, are able to work as "symbolic analysts"?

History teaches us, however, that merely assuming a continuation of recent trends is often very misleading. Technology is less like a railroad track than a spiral staircase, with many reversals of direction along its upward path. The long-term effect of the Industrial Revolution is a case in point. To Victorian futurists, it seemed obvious that the capital-using bias of industrial technology would continue indefinitely, bringing with it an ever-greater gulf between the owners of capital and the working class. In *The Time Machine* (1895) H. G. Wells forecast a future in which workers have been reduced to subhuman status. These Victorians were wrong—indeed, if Wells had possessed the kind of data available today, he would have known that wages had begun to rise again long before he wrote his novel. During the 20th century, capital has claimed a declining share of the national income and labor has taken a growing share.

Technological advance, moreover, does not always increase the need for skilled labor. On the contrary, in the past one of the main effects of mechanization was to reduce the special skills required to carry out many tasks. It took considerable skill and experience to weave cloth on a hand loom, but just about anybody could learn to tend a power loom. What is true is that, to date, technological progress has consistently tended to increase the demand for a particular kind of skill, the kind that is taught in formal education and is most easily acquired by the kind of person who does well in formal education. Two centuries ago, only a minority of jobs required literacy; one century ago, only a few jobs required anything like a modern college education. Nowadays higher education is not a luxury for the wealthy but something intensely practical, a virtual necessity for the career minded.

But it is not at all clear that this trend will continue indefinitely. There is no inherent reason why technology cannot be "college-education saving" rather than college-education using. It is possible to see examples of how this might occur even today. This essay, for example, was written using a newly acquired word processor. I did not bother to read the manual; the graphical interface, with its menus of icons, usually makes it obvious how to do what I want, and I can easily call up on-screen help with the push of a button if I get lost. Whenever we use the term "user friendly," we are implying that we have a production technique that requires less skill than it used to.

But isn't this kind of reversal always going to be the exception rather than the rule? Not necessarily. In fact, I would make a speculative argument that in the long run technology will tend to devalue the work of "symbolic analysts" and favor the talents that are common to all human beings. After all, even the most brilliant specialists are actually rather poor at formal reasoning, while even the most ordinary person can carry out feats of informal information processing that remain far beyond the reach of the most powerful computers. As the artificial intelligence pioneer Marvin Minsky points out, "A 1956 program solved hard problems in mathematical logic, and a 1961 program solved college-level problems in calculus. Yet not until the 1970s could we construct robot programs that could see and move well enough to arrange children's building blocks into simple towers.... What people vaguely call common sense is actually more intricate than most of the technical expertise we admire." Chess-playing programs are not yet quite good enough to beat the world's greatest players, but they are getting there; a program that can recognize faces as well as a two-year-old can remains a distant dream.

Rereading *Player Piano* recently, I found the totally automated factories Vonnegut imagined more than 40 years ago completely credible, but found myself wondering who cleans them (or for that matter the houses of his industrial elite)? It is no accident that no description is given of how these mundane tasks are automated—because as Vonnegut must have sensed, it will be a very long time before we know how to build a machine equipped with the ordinary human common sense to do what we usually regard as simple tasks.

So here is a speculation: The time may come when most tax lawyers are replaced by expert systems software, but human beings are still needed—and well paid—for such truly difficult occupations as gardening, house cleaning, and the thousands of other services that will receive an ever-growing share of our expenditure as mere consumer goods become steadily cheaper. The high-skill professions whose members have done so well during the last 20 years may turn out to be the modern counterpart of early-19th-century weavers, whose incomes soared after the mechanization of spinning, only to crash when the technological revolution reached their own craft.

I suspect, then, that the current era of growing inequality and the devaluation of ordinary work will turn out to be only a temporary phase. In some sufficiently long run the tables will be turned: Those uncommon skills that are rare because they are so unnatural will be largely taken over or made easy by computers, while machines will still be unable to do what every person can. In other words, I predict that the current age of inequality will give way to a golden age of *equality*. In the very long run, of course, the machines will be able to do everything we can. By that time, however, it will be *their* responsibility to take care of the problem.

Note

1. For a fuller discussion of this point, see my article in the *Harvard Business Review* (Summer 1994). In a comprehensive survey of the literature on job creation, *High and Persistent Unemployment: Assessment of the Problem and its Causes* (1993), economist Jørgen Elmeskov flatly concludes that "trade seems an unlikely prime candidate for explaining increased unemployment."

13   The Localization of
        the World Economy

Most people find economics a terribly confusing subject—all
the more so when the talk turns to the mysteries of international trade and finance. We all, understandably, look for something that gives us a vivid picture; and so we usually turn to
the stories of individual businesses—of companies that have
succeeded or failed in the international marketplace.

Unfortunately, such stories are all too often misleading. It's
not just that General Motors, whatever it may think, is not
representative of the American economy. No matter which
company you study, indeed no matter how many companies
you study, you won't be getting the full picture—because the
economy is more than the sum of its parts. To make sense of
the way our economy is changing, we need to understand how
producers and consumers interact, which is something no accumulation of competitive war stories can convey.

And yet the economy as a whole is simply too big, too
remote from ordinary experience, to grasp. Is there any piece
of the economy that can truly help us understand the whole?

I suggest a somewhat unusual answer, but one that is growing in popularity among economists: That a particularly good

Reprinted by permission from *New Perspectives Quarterly* (Winter 1995):
34–38.

way to understand the American economy is by studying American cities. Specifically, this essay is a tale of two such cities, separated in time and space: Chicago a century ago and Los Angeles today. Each of those cities ballooned in half a century from little more than a village into a huge metropolis. Each of them was, in its prime, arguably the quintessential American city, embodying in its energy, in its style, even in its problems much of what was most characteristic of our society and especially our economy. And the comparison between them is the best way I know to explain some of the often misunderstood realities of the American economy and its place in the world.

Think of old Chicago and new LA, and you will probably come up with some immediate contrasts that sound like the sort of thing you always hear about the economy: snowbelt versus sunbelt, heartland versus Pacific Rim. But these are superficial observations, catchphrases rather than real economic analysis. To really learn something, we have to dig a little deeper.

Perhaps the most surprising things that you find when you compare Chicago 1894 with Los Angeles 1994 are not the differences but the similarities. Both were gigantic boomtowns, in which a kind of chain reaction of growth transformed villages into huge metropolitan areas in less than a single life-time. Both were immigrant cities: If modern LA seems to some Anglos like a foreign country, what would they have thought of Chicago where in 1900 half of the residents were foreign born?

Chicago then and LA now were also, of course, cities in which great wealth coexisted with massive poverty, in which optimism about human progress was continually challenged by social ills. Old Chicago certainly gets the worst of the comparison: Despite its growing underclass, despite its gangs and drug wars, LA has not at least so far fallen back into the depths that Chicago's social workers described.

Perhaps most surprising is the way that both cities were integrated into a worldwide web of trade and finance. It is a late 20th-century conceit that we invented the global economy just yesterday. We read stories about Boeing dueling with Airbus, Japanese investors buying New York real estate, BMW opening a plant in South Carolina, or world stock markets quivering on news from Europe; and we imagine that we live in an unprecedented global village. Surely our great-grand-fathers could not have conceived of a world grown so small! And yet a century ago Chicago meatpackers were acutely aware of their competition with New Zealand. The railroads that converged on the city, bringing beef and wheat destined for European markets, were largely built with European capital—indeed, on the eve of the First World War Great Britain's overseas investments were larger than its domestic capital stock, a record no major country has ever come close to matching since. The chemical companies that provided old Chicago with dyes for its fabrics and aspirin for its headaches were primarily multinationals with headquarters in Germany. And the Chicago futures market was every bit as sensitive to news of droughts in the Ukraine and frost in Brazil as it is today. To be sure, international money transfers took a few hours instead of a millisecond, and one did not decide to make an overnight trip to Buenos Aires on two days' notice. In terms of the serious substance of economic affairs, however, Chicago 1894 was arguably as much a part of a global market as Los Angeles today. We all know that modern technologies are what make a truly global economy possible; but it turns out that the key enabling technologies were the steam engine and the telegraph.

Politics Kills

Incidentally, if this was true, why do we imagine that the global market is something new? Because politics killed that first global economy. Between 1914 and 1945 wars and protectionism tore up the dense web of trade, investment and often family ties that linked old Chicago to the rest of the world. In some ways the world has never recovered. It is a little-known but startling fact that world trade as a share of world production did not return to its 1913 level until about 1970; it is even more startling that net international flows of capital (as opposed to complex financial operations that do not finance real investment) were a considerably larger share of world savings in the years preceding World War I than they have been even in the "emerging market" boom of the last few years. Surely everyone who thinks about it is aware that for all our current hysteria, international migration was far larger in an era that could actually build the Statue of Liberty to welcome immigrants than it has ever been since.

Despite all these similarities, however, it is clear that the economy of Los Angeles today is very different from the economy of Chicago, or any other city, a century ago. But what is the nature of that difference?

I would suggest that the most striking difference (aside from the immense improvement in the average standard of living) is what we might call the abstractness of the modern city's economy—the way it seems so disconnected from the physical world.

Consider, for example, the most basic question about a city: Where is it, and why is it in that location? Look at a railway map of the United States a century ago, and you will have no trouble understanding why Chicago was a great metropolis. Chicago was the city the railroads made: It was the place where the rail lines of the outer Midwest converged, like an immense root system gathering nutrients to feed the great trunk lines (as they were actually called) leading East. And while it may not have been inevitable that Chicago would be the site at which the resources of the heartland would be ingathered, the southwest corner of Lake Michigan was a fairly obvious place to locate the city that the historian William Cronon has called "Nature's Metropolis."

By contrast, why put America's Second City in the Los Angeles Basin? There was once oil there, but it's gone now. It was once a good place to make movies, because of the clear air and good weather; but nowadays movies are made indoors or on location, and anyway the air is smoggy. It was once a good place to build airplanes, when they were assembled out of doors and test-flown on the spot, but these days aircraft are built in factories, and the air traffic controllers would not appreciate it if you took a casual spin over LAX. Try to understand why any of LA's most characteristic industries are there now, as opposed to how they got started, and you always find a circular argument: The film studios are there because of the large pool of people with specialized skills, and the skilled people are there because it's where the jobs are. (By the way, there's nothing wrong with circular arguments in economic geography).

The economy of Los Angeles, then, seems to have cut loose from its geographical moorings: Most of the things the city does for a living could, it seems, be done anywhere. The 3 million people of Chicago 1894 were there because Chicago was the gateway to the heartland; they were there because of the farms, forests, and mines in the city's hinterland. The 11 million people of modern LA are there because of each other; if one could uproot the whole city and move it 500 miles, the economic base would hardly be affected.

But in any case, what is that economic base? What did Chicago do for a living then, and what does LA do now?

Well, Carl Sandburg summed it up for old Chicago: "hog-butcher to the world." And also, of course, lumber merchant, wheat trader, manufacturer of farm machinery, oil refiner, steel-maker. Chicago 1894 was a city that made or transported things, and all you had to do was walk around the city to get a pretty good idea of its role in the national and world economy.

But what exactly does LA do? Aside from some of the people who work in dream factories, the working people of Los Angeles look pretty much like working people anywhere else; the buildings in which they work and live, indeed the whole city looks like anywhere else (or perhaps it would be better to say that these days every place looks a lot like LA). Stare at the streams of white-collar workers pouring in and out of the office buildings in the suburban malls, and you would be hard put to say how the economy of Los Angeles is different from that of any other major U.S. metropolis. Again, the city's economy seems strangely detached from any sense of place.

Why is the LA world of work so undistinctive in appearance? You might be tempted to say that it is because the city has a highly diversified economy—that the Los Angeles economy "looks like America" not just in the clothes it wears but in the things it makes. But that isn't quite right—a lesson the severe recession of recent years should have taught us. Regional economists like to make distinction between a region's "export base"—the goods and services it sells to people in other regions, inside or outside the U.S.—and the "non-base" workers, the insurance agents, fast-food servers and dentists who sell their products to customers nearby. Well, it turns out that the export base of Los Angeles is, in fact, highly special-ized. Despite the city's immensity, it is highly dependent on a few key industries: entertainment, defense, aerospace. That is why Southern California proved so vulnerable in this last recession: when a slump in world aircraft orders coincided with sharp cuts in defense spending, the whole region went into a tailspin.

If the city is so specialized, however, why isn't that more obvious to the causal observer? One answer is that workers themselves have become less distinctive. A century ago, a Chicago meatpacker wore different clothes from those of a New York garment worker, had a different physique and could be identified by sight (or other senses, if you were downwind). Today an aerospace worker in Los Angeles looks pretty much the same as a pharmaceutical worker in New Jersey. Again, it's part of the growing abstractness of the economy.

But there's another reason, which surprisingly few people seem to understand. It is that while Los Angeles sells a surprisingly narrow range of goods and services to the world at large, most people in LA don't sell their wares to distant customers. Instead, most of the employment is in those "non-base" activities, goods and (especially) services that are provided by local workers, to local consumers, for local consumption. And since the kinds of things that we consume—the services of shopping mall clerks, of lawyers, of chiropractors, of school-teachers—are pretty much the same wherever you go, there is a sense in which the economy of Los Angeles "looks like America" after all.

But wasn't that true of Chicago a century ago? Not to the same extent. Although we talk a lot these days about globalization, about a world grown small, when you look at the economies of modern cities what you see is a process of localization: A steadily rising share of the work force produces services that are sold only within that same metropolitan area. In 1894 Chicago's base employment was probably more than half the total—that is, more than half the workers were hog-butchers, steelworkers, etc., making the distinctive wares Chicago sold to the world. In Los Angeles today that fraction is probably no more than a quarter.

Localization

This process of localization explains what would otherwise seem a paradox about the world economy: The fact that international trade is not much bigger now, as a share of world output, than it was a century ago. Here are some statistics: in 1993, the United States spent 11 percent of its income on imports. In 1890 the corresponding figure was eight percent. That's not much of an increase, especially when you consider that during the 19th century the U.S. was frankly protectionist, while today it is a relatively open market. And other countries did an extraordinary amount of trade: Great Britain exported some 40 percent of its gross domestic product in the 1850s, more than it does today. And yet we read all the time about how modern transportation and communication have made it possible to "explode the value-added chain"—for Taiwanese workers to take an American microprocessor, wire it up to a disk drive made in Singapore, put the whole thing in a plastic case made in China and ship it back to America. Why doesn't all this to-ing and fro-ing lead to vastly more trade than the more prosaic manufacturing processes of the late 19th century? Because while we ship manufactured goods back and forth with unprecedented abandon, such "tradeables" constitute a steadily shrinking share of our economy.

This is not an accident: It is a trend that is deeply rooted in the nature of economic and technical change.

Start with a first, seemingly paradoxical principle: The kinds of jobs that grow over time are not the things we do well but the things we do badly. The American economy has become supremely efficient at growing food; as a result, we are able to feed ourselves and a good part of the rest of the world while employing only two percent of the work force on the farm. On the other hand, it takes as many people to serve a meal or man a cash register as it always did; that's why so many of the jobs our economy creates are in food service and retail trade. Industries that achieve rapid productivity growth tend to lose jobs, not gain them.

But where has our economy achieved its most rapid productivity growth? One answer is that we are getting better and better at producing goods—food, clothing, autos—but not improving very much at providing services. An even better answer would be that we are making rapid progress in fields where the information required is relatively easy to formalize, to embody in a set of instructions to a robot or a computer; we have made much less progress in activities, from cutting hair to medical care, where the information processing is of the exceedingly subtle and extremely complex kind that we call common sense.

But the kinds of activities that we can't program a computer or robot to do for us, that require the human touch, also typically require direct human contact. That is, precisely because farming, manufacturing and some impersonal services have become so productive, our economy increasingly focuses on the other things—the "nontradeable" activities that make up the "non-base" employment that occupies most people in modern cities. And that's why most people in Los Angeles produce services for local consumption, and therefore do pretty much the same things as most people in metropolitan New York— or for that matter in London, Paris and modern Chicago.

This, finally, brings us to the moral of the story. You will find a lot of people who are worried about the American economy. That's reasonable: We have plenty of real problems.

But many of these people seem to be worried for the wrong reasons. They worry, for example, about "deindustrialization:" Where, they ask, have all the manufacturing jobs gone? And they look at our strangely abstract economy and worry that its prosperity is somehow unsound, that (in the words of the recent World Competitiveness Report) we are "rich in consumption but not in production."

But consider Los Angeles. It is not very obviously a manufacturing city; but it is actually somewhat more manufacturing oriented than other big American cities, and if we had statistics we would probably find that it exports more manufactures than it imports. It is not a city where many people produce anything tangible; but that is precisely because its residents are so good at the tangible stuff that their energy is focused on the intangibles. You should not, in other words, fault Los Angeles 1994 for not looking like Chicago 1894.

Now LA has, of course, just suffered a severe recession. Economists who specialize in these things tell me that the slump was mostly just bad luck, and they expect a strong recovery. Nonetheless, it may be that the growth of Los Angeles will slow: Perhaps the technology of the 21st century will favor another kind of city, or maybe the process of abstraction will allow us to do away with cities altogether. But if you focus neither on the very short run not on the speculative future, what you see in Los Angeles is an economy that, like that of the United States, relates to the rest of the world in a way that is sometimes hard to grasp, but basically sensible and sound; the wealth of the city and the country is far more solid than the abstractness of the economy might lead you to fear.

So next time someone tries to frighten you with the fear of global competition, and tries to prove his point by telling you about closing factories and declining manufacturing, consider the contrast between old Chicago and modern LA, and remind him: "I have seen the present, and it works!"

Index